TETRASCROLL

TETRA

GOLDILOCKS AN

A Cosmic Fairy Tale

SCROLL

O THE THREE BEARS

oy R. Buckminster Fuller

ULAE, Inc./St. Martin's Press

Library of Congress Cataloging in Publication Data

Fuller, R. Buckminster (Richard Buckminster), 1895-
    Tetrascroll.

    1. Fuller, R. Buckminster (Richard Buckminster),
1895-   . Tetrascroll—Illustrations. 2. Artists'
books—United States. I. Title.
NE2312.F85A4 1982   769.92′4   82-777
ISBN 0-312-79362-6   AACR2
ISBN 0-312-79363-4 (special deluxe ed.)

Design by Manuela Paul
10   9   8   7   6   5   4   3   2   1
First Edition

TABLE OF CONTENTS

PROLOGUE

One day in 1930, when our daughter Allegra was three years old, she said, "Daddy, tell me about Goldilocks and the Three Bears." The story had been read to her many times from a child's illustrated book. As I started telling it, I began to think of new and heretofore unknown details of the famous story. Allegra was delighted with the innovations. From time to time she would ask me to tell her the story again. Gradually, with new insights into their characters, both Goldy and the Three Bears became much more interesting personalities as may the personalities in the comic strips.

At that time I was studying Einstein and others whose work promised to revolutionize the frontiers of thought. One day, when Allegra asked me to tell her a Goldilocks story, I decided to try out a scientific seminar conducted by Goldy with the Three Bears as students asking pertinent questions and getting lucid answers and explanations from Goldy. This intrigued Allegra much more than facetious behavior on the part of the bears and Goldy.

After the bears and Goldy made ice cream sodas and were comfortably seated in their famous chairs—with Goldy in a new portable movie director's chair—they would start talking about this and that, which would always lead to the most scientifically and philosophically challenging subjects. But the bears and Goldy never called it science or mathematics.

This was the beginning of my spontaneous thinking-out-loud discourses such as I now give publicly.

I became convinced that through imagined expansion of the recallable inventory of fundamental experiences of the child, achieved through description of analogous experiences of others, altered only in magnitude and always similar in principle to the child's experience recalls, it would be possible to effectively induce that child's discovery of the most complex and profound phenomena.

I was also convinced that the best way to study the thoughts of the scientists I was reading was to test myself by disclosing what I understood to a child. This also put the scientist, whose thoughts I was relaying, under great test. The scientist must be elegantly logical to the child, or else the scientist's logic is questionable.

My out-loud thinking sought for the generalized principles common to all the special-case experiences—principles of orderly variation of interrelationships between special-case experiences not implicit in or inferred from any integral characteristics of any of the special cases when each is considered only separately. Next I must induce the child to imagine making her own natural objective use of those subjectively discovered principles. I felt it to be true that children had great advantage in this respect as they are not burdened with the misconceptions and obsolete propositions with which the grown-ups have been inundated by formal "education."

Thus began a six-year series of discourses. School lessons and other events gradually and imperceptibly shunted aside the stories. One day in 1939 Allegra came home from school a little weary and sat down to relax. Suddenly she looked at me and said, hesitatingly, "Daddy, one more Goldilocks story?" And that was the last time. We both knew that a wonderful chapter in life's book had been completed. We had gained a great deal from those spontaneously initiated ventures into approximately every field of experience, speculation, and disciplined thought. But we no longer needed the fictitious self-starter. From then on the main engines kept going on their own. The integrity and spontaneity of our thinking was not compromised.

Now Allegra is a great dance-anthropologist and chairone of the department of dance in the University of California at Los Angeles. Allegra will go on dancing forever because, as Goldy says, "Dance is the language of Universe."

Bucky and daughter, Allegra

From time to time I as yet hear from Goldy, and she asks that on the occasion of Anne's and my fifty-eighth wedding anniversary and my eightieth birthday, we dedicate to Allegra Goldy's résumé of her latest illustrated cosmic seminar, to which she has given the title *Tetrascroll.*

INTRODUCTION

by Amei Wallach

In the spring of 1975, when she was not yet seventy-one, Tatyana Grosman began telling friends that her latest project involved "a young man, and I can't keep up with him." The young man was R. Buckminster Fuller. Working with Tatyana Grosman was his eightieth-birthday present.

Our present, too, it turns out, because the result of that improbable celebration is this book. *Tetrascroll* is for that 100 percent of humanity whom Tatyana Grosman regards as hungry for an experience that is both pure and beautiful. And it is for that 99 percent of humanity Buckminster Fuller calculates does not understand science, for the simple reason that most scientists are so awkward in explaining their world.

Buckminster Fuller has no such difficulties. Half a century ago he figured out how to explain Einstein and Eddington to his three-year-old daughter, Allegra. And now he is using that same technique to explain Buckminster Fuller to us. Synergy is at the heart of Buckminster Fuller's findings, but synergy defined in a way it has never been defined

before. Buckminster Fuller's synergy is a science of relationships. The behavior of whole systems, he says, cannot be predicted by the behavior of individual systems acting alone. The difference lies in what happens between them when they interact. *Tetrascroll* is what happened in the interaction between two formidable systems named Buckminster Fuller and Tatyana Grosman. The story of *Tetrascroll*'s making is the story of that relationship. It is the story of Bucky and Tanya.

Despite their venerable years, awesome accomplishments, and a certain unstated imperiousness of manner, Buckminster Fuller immediately becomes "Bucky" to just about everyone who meets him, and Tatyana Grosman is simply "Tanya." To everyone, that is, except the principals themselves. Throughout their creative adventure Tanya addressed Bucky as "Dr. Fuller" and he called her "Tatyana," "My Dear," or both, as in, "Tatyana, My Dear."

But for most of us the diminutive suits them, and this has something to do with the childlike directness and wonder with which each regards the world. In many ways every day is a birthday for both of them, a new day to start all over again, at the very beginning. A day to test and explore.

Tanya's realm is fine art as manifested in the process of printmaking. Bucky's is science—and philosophy, and poetry, and architecture, and mathematics, and technology, and metaphysics. Together they have brought forth a children's book, a fable that requires intense concentration for an adult to fully understand. Children, with minds uncluttered by years of wrongheaded learning, will have an easier time with *Tetrascroll* than will many of their parents. The way to read this book is to remember Bucky's advice: "See the drawings like a child. Do the drawings have meaning for a child?"

Bucky calls the book "everything I think and feel in mathematics and philosophy and everything else." For Tanya it is "a very beautiful achievement by an artist, a pure vision expressed in lithography."

In its original incarnation *Tetrascroll* was a lithographic book-object that consisted of twenty-six pages bound together by the sturdy Dacron that is most commonly used in sailmaking. Each page was a thirty-six-inch equilateral triangle—one of the four faces of the tetrahedron, which Bucky has established as the basic unit in nature. Each triangular page contained text and one of Bucky's engaging drawings, which he had executed with crayon and pencil on lithographic stone. The pages were hinged to one another in such a way that they unfolded into any number of forms, including a circle. *Tetrascroll* could be spread out to a forty-foot strip, or it could be

unfurled like a scroll at each end. *Tetrascroll* was first presented to the public on January 29, 1977, when it was exhibited in two of its possible forms at the Museum of Modern Art and at Ronald Feldman Fine Arts, a Manhattan gallery that specializes in the avant garde. The way the museum hung the book, it stretched across one wall, then, turning the corner, continued on an adjacent wall. At Feldman *Tetrascroll* lay face up on platforms set out in the middle of the gallery, like two sides of a massive triangle. As art, it was displayed in both places, and as art *Tetrascroll* was emphatically meant to be enjoyed. Still, at those January, 1977 openings, the guests discarded the habitual rite of socializing to concentrate closely on the text. Even in its guise of a deluxe art object limited to an edition of thirty-four, *Tetrascroll* was every bit a book meant for reading.

From the first, Bucky had intended that *Tetrascroll* should be available for a wider audience. He appreciated the exacting discipline of making beautiful lithographs at Tanya's print workshop, Universal Limited Art Editions—and also her insistence on limiting each page of an edition to what a printer can print in a single day. For Tanya each page must be the expression of one day's touch, its atmosphere and psychological state—unaltered by differences in weather, or family affairs, or whether or not breakfast was agreeable.

Bucky relished the intuitive and artistic in which everyone at ULAE had concentrated on his book. "Everyone was completely enchanted as the story unfolded itself," he said on the day of the Museum of Modern Art opening. "Really, it unfolded itself like *Tetrascroll* unfolds." But he wanted his million readers—not to mention everyone else—to be able to enjoy the story too. More than enjoy. Bucky is sure *Tetrascroll*'s message is vital if man is to make a success of himself. Besides, the words that appeared in the original *Tetrascroll* were only part of what he had to say. They were words distilled from a larger text, which appears in this version of the book interspersed with the twenty-one lithographs and their captions ("tricaps"), which contain the text from the original art-object *Tetrascroll*. Bucky wanted a commercial edition of the book, and Tanya and her studio manager, Bill Goldston, obliged by arranging a joint publication with Bucky's commercial publisher, St. Martin's Press. This edition of *Tetrascroll* is the first book co-published by ULAE, Inc. and a trade publisher.

Since 1956 lithography has been the primary concern of Universal Limited Art Editions, where Tanya presides. With stones discovered on her doorway path and a secondhand press purchased for fifteen dollars, ULAE began producing limited-edition lithographs of such precision, care, and lavish inventiveness that the studio helped revive the art of printmaking in the United States and earned itself a reputation as one of the finest print workshops in the world. After twenty-five years of publication Tanya, as Bucky had before her, won the coveted Brandeis Notable Achievement Award for "Genius, artistic excellence and notable accomplishment."

The list of artists who have worked at ULAE includes many who had no public at all when Tanya first found them. Now, however, it reads like a condensed "Who's Who" of American art: Lee Bontecou, Jim Dine, Sam Francis, Helen Frankenthaler, Fritz Glarner, Jasper Johns, Alexander Liberman, Marisol, Robert Motherwell, Barnett Newman, Claes Oldenburg, Robert Rauschenberg, Larry Rivers, James Rosenquist, Saul Steinberg, Cy Twombly. Through a gift from Armand and Celeste Bartos, the Museum of Modern Art acquires number one of every edition of lithographs—and etchings and woodcuts—that the studio prints. And museums and galleries around the world are anxious to be first to display the latest ULAE accomplishment.

Bucky knew nothing of ULAE's reputation in February, 1975, when his young friend Edwin Schlossberg suggested they visit the white frame house at 5 Skidmore Place in West Islip, Long Island, where Tanya and her presses reside. Bucky's investigations into nature, technology, and the universe had in the past led him into byways like anthropology and poetry. His findings had already affected biology, medicine, physics, technology, and architecture. But never before had he had a great deal to do with the world of fine arts.

Tanya was aware in only the haziest way of Buckminster Fuller. She had heard something. That he was an engineer, an architect. Something. But Eddie Schlossberg they both knew, and well. Tanya had met the tall, tousle-haired poet-physicist in 1966, when he was twenty years old, a Columbia University undergraduate. He had come with Jasper Johns to watch the artist work at ULAE. Tanya asked the composed young man what he did, and when he said that he made poems, she asked to see his work. The result: *Wordswordswords,* an unbound, limited edition book of Schlossberg's poems, printed in different ways on different materials. Some sheets are embossed, some etched, some pressed onto the back of the paper and meant to be read through the paper, some typed on sheets of aluminum, or black paper, or plastic, or regular typing bond. Options and alternatives.

Options and alternatives are at the core of Bucky's vision, too. There are thirty different relationships in a tetrahedron. Recognizing the possibilities will make it possible for us to survive. Although Bucky and Schlossberg were born a full half-century apart within a July week of one another, the two men have much in common. So much, in fact, that in the early months of their friendship, when Schlossberg was twenty-four and a doctoral candidate in physics and literature, Bucky had found himself irked—"miffed" is the word he uses—at the letters Schlossberg wrote him. Eddie's words and thoughts so closely resembled Bucky's own that the younger man seemed to be aping the older. But after a while Bucky realized it was simply that they were so much alike that thinking and talking in a Fulleresque way came naturally to Schlossberg. At Southern Illinois University, where Bucky was Distinguished University Professor in the 1960s, Schlossberg helped him develop the World Game. The game offers a way of organizing data about the world's resources and then suggesting hundreds, thousands of alternatives for dispersing them.

In 1975 Bucky would be eighty years old, and Schlossberg would be thirty. He wanted to give Bucky something special for his birthday. Most special of all for a creative man, Schlossberg decided, would be "something new to do." Something new to do at Tanya's.

With that end in mind Schlossberg rummaged in the Buckminster Fuller archives at the University City Science Center in Philadelphia, where Bucky has been World Fellow in Residence since 1972. Every scrap of paper, every contract, every note, every drawing that has ever crossed the redoubtable World Fellow's path is housed there. Schlossberg rolled together drawings of such Fuller inventions as the three-wheeled Dymaxion car, the cable-suspended circular Dymaxion house, and the geodesic dome. He threw in a childish scrawl or two out of Bucky's faraway past and then dispatched the bundle to Tanya.

She was baffled. She has no idea what to do with these puzzling "blueprints," as she called them. "I was absolutely helpless looking at this material," she remembers. "I couldn't understand the connection from one drawing to another, or even why the drawings were done."

In the midst of all that arcana, however, were three drawings of a child. They looked as if one person had penciled in the outlines, someone else had colored them in, and a third person had written the captions with the uncertain lettering of a child. In fact, Bucky had drawn the outlines; his wife, Anne Hewlett Fuller, had colored them in; their daughter, Allegra, had written the captions underneath. Tanya's favorite depicted a sneezing child who was identified as "Bugs" in a bold, wavering hand. She returned the "blueprints" to Schlossberg, kept the drawings, and awaited Bucky's arrival for tea.

It was bright on the afternoon of Tuesday, February 25, 1975. And cold. The wind howled petulantly all day, and would the next. In the passenger seat of Schlossberg's Volvo Bucky was playing the Milton Berle trick that has made it possible for him to go with a minimum of sleep for more than fifty years. He laid his head on his shoulder and snapped into a cat nap, leaving Schlossberg to contend with the traffic, which, as usual on Long Island, was hopelessly snarled.

It was 5:00 in the afternoon by the time they arrived. White linen napkins had been placed over the plates of food which Mrs. Jones, the ULAE cook (a Frenchwoman despite her name), had long since prepared when the two men stepped onto the wooden porch and into the small front room that doubles as ULAE archive and reception hall.

As usual, Bucky was wearing a dark suit. As usual, Tanya was elegant and erect as she motioned the men to the small, round table covered with white linen and lace and with the culinary delights with which she habitually greets her guests. Food is an important part of the ULAE ritual. Bucky declined everything but the tea, which he drinks incessantly and in a quantity that easily qualifies him for the "enraptured fireplug" description his biographer Hugh Kenner once employed in an article for *The New York Times*.

In repose, when he is not smiling, Bucky can resemble a rather clubby and humorless banker. His head is high and domed, his hazel eyes bland behind thick glasses, and his square chin folds in on itself like origami paper. Then he grins, and suddenly he is approachable, animated, and instantly recognizable as the foremost living practitioner of the four-hour, five-hour, ten-hour marathon talk. Bucky also happens to be decidedly squat. During all his time at ULAE he managed to forego all culinary pleasures except steak, spinach, and Jell-O. With that menu, repeated three times a day, he had reduced from a high of 206 pounds of too solid flesh, and with that menu he intended to maintain his accomplishment.

Most biographers say that Buckminster Fuller stands about five feet, two inches tall. While he agrees that he is "short by twentieth-century dimensions," he asserts his height is five-six. Tanya, who is definitely diminutive at five-two, says she believes that she is taller than "this great man." She is, however, slight to the point of delicacy.

Her face is small and softly pointed at the chin, and it wears a glow. Sometimes she tilts her chin expectantly; sometimes she firmly sets it straight. The eyes above are soft and vulnerable. She speaks softly, too, in a generously accented English derivative of Russian, and it is necessary to lean forward and listen hard in order to understand her.

Bucky talks forcefully and intemperately at a rate he estimates at 7,000 words per hour. The words tumble out, stumbling over one another, as he gulps for breath in odd places, the better to hold tight to a phrase at the end, thus forestalling any unforeseen interruptions before his thought has run its often convoluted course. His accent is that of upper-class New England. He often speaks in a chairman-of-the-board, matter-of-fact slur that makes it easy to miss whole paragraphs of what he is saying. Bucky is also rather deaf, a malady

"Tatyana, my dear." "Dr. Fuller."

only partially offset by the hearing aids he wears in each ear.

On that first day, in February of 1975, before Bucky and Tanya had learned the rhythms of each other's speech or intuited the patterns that would render their words intelligible to one another, it was Schlossberg who interpreted. He sat between them at the small, round table, ear toward Tanya's mouth, mouth toward Bucky's ear, back and forth like a spectator at a tennis match. Not that there was anything the least competitive in the encounter.

There might have been. Bucky is accustomed to absolute monarchy in any space he occupies, benevolent as that dominion may be. Tanya's way is clear to herself, and she is practiced in the art of teasing, cajoling, inspiring, and goading her artists into the paths she is sure will lead them right. But between Bucky and Tanya, those who watched have said, there was immediate and courtly respect.

The meeting had come at a difficult moment for Bucky. In just a month *Synergetics*—the book that provides the underlying structure for Bucky's lifetime of mathematical and scientific contributions—would be published. It had taken some fifty-two years of fits and starts, of articles here, talks everywhere, fourteen books on phases of the subject, and a nagging reminder provided by a locked, black briefcase crammed with manuscript pages. But R. Buckminster Fuller had finally completed his life's work.

With the help of his logical and persistent friend, E. J. Applewhite, Bucky had at last laid out in writing the mathematical formulae and empirical observations on which he based his concept that all physical and metaphysical experience could be described in terms of a tetrahedron—that four-sided triangular configuration that Bucky is sure is the primary building block of nature and the universe. *Synergetics*—"Bucky's *Principia*," as it has since come to be called—was due to be published on April 3, 1975, and Bucky's friends felt some concern about him.

They were not yet aware that, his brain now unburdened of its accumulated eight decades of thought, Bucky would begin all over again, spinning out new inventiveness that would result in still more ideas, still newer books, including *Synergetics 2*. They knew only that after rewriting the last of the galleys for the original *Synergetics* Bucky had confessed to Applewhite that he felt disoriented. The exhilaration of unwinding from himself that lifetime-evolved skein of formulae, diagrams, models, tables, numbers, and

"The behavior of whole systems cannot be predicted by the behavior of individual systems acting alone."

words had come undone. The focus of his inexhaustible energy was gone, and Bucky was somewhat at a loss. Schlossberg hoped Tanya would be the answer.

In West Islip, on the first day of their meeting, Tanya and Bucky sat for a time at the table in ULAE's front room. Besides the nineteenth-century country chairs on which they sat, only prints and cabinets furnish the room. The floor is bare, the feeling spare. There are three doors in the room. One leads to the front stairs, one to the back office and kitchen, and one next door to what was once the garage of the house and is now the workshop in which the prints are made. Bucky and Tanya talked, and then Bill Goldston, who is the ULAE studio manager, and Tony Towle, a poet and for many years Tanya's secretary, led the way upstairs to the immaculate viewing room. There, making a ceremony of it, they brought out some of the books ULAE has printed. Silently and carefully they turned each page. There was Schlossberg's *Wordswordswords,* Barnett Newman's *18 Cantos,* and Robert Motherwell's *A la Pintura.* Of the last, curator John J. McKendry had written in the catalog introduction for its Metropolitan Museum exhibit, "Motherwell has concentrated so much of his creativity into these pages that if all of his paintings, and other works, were destroyed, if only this book were to survive, Motherwell would still be seen as a major artist of the Twentieth Century."

It wasn't too long after he began looking at the work, that Bucky called for a stone of his own. By the time Towle ended his day at 6:40, he was able to note in his diary: "Dr.

Fuller is just drawing one of his domes on a stone with a No. 5 crayon."

As a child Bucky had loved drawing with charcoal. But his mother informed him that the men of their family became doctors and lawyers and ministers, and in 1905 he put away his drawing tools—those lovely tools. He had drawn diagrams since then, with a pen or pencil, taking care to be completely accurate. But this unrehearsed, pure concentration on line and feeling in Tanya's studio was new. In fact, he pronounced it "thrilling."

That first drawing of a dome did not appear in the original book, and it has not been reproduced in this one. But it served its purpose. In the past Tanya had enticed unwilling artists to try the stone. ("I began lithography reluctantly, thinking the second half of the 20th century was no time to start writing on rocks," Robert Rauschenberg has written of his first, fateful encounter with Tanya.) She had grown adept at angling. This time she had hooked her big one without even trying. The work had begun. What happened next for Bucky and Tanya came out of their respective gifts, and their strengths, and the sum of their lives.

Buckminster Fuller and Tatyana Grosman are, as Bucky might say, simultaneous events, each encapsulating an important if finite chunk of history. He, the quintessential Yankee, descended from Puritans and Transcendentalists, married another Yankee, Anne Hewlett, whose families on both sides were among the original settlers of Long Island. The newspapers called it a wedding of "mothball aristocracy," Bucky still tells with glee.

Tanya, the inward, extravagant Russian, resonating to Chekhov's pauses and Pushkin's poems, married an improvident, exuberant artist, Maurice Grosman. It was the first test of her indomitable will. Her family disliked the match. She took a solitary ski trip to decide, and returned to break with them.

Bucky imbibed the principles of practical experience during boyhood summers sailing off Bear Island in Maine's Penobscot Bay, where, he wrote in his book, *Ideas and Integrities,* "boat building is the parent technology." There he learned an early intimacy with "such tension systems as seines, trawls, weirs, scallop drags, lobster pot heads, and traps together with all their respective drag and buoy gear" and practiced with "stout cordage and light lines" the techniques of "net-weaving, tying, splicing, and serving."

Tanya's girlhood memories are of the drama of despair then playing out its final act in Russia, where she was born on June 30, 1904. Her hometown was Ekaterinburg, where later Czar Nicholas II and his family were to be shot. While the men played cards in their clubs on somnolent afternoons, a revolution was going on. Prisoners on their way to incarceration in a wing of her father's house which had been commandeered for that purpose were lost along the way, fallen or pushed into mine shafts, where they could be heard singing for days, until the sound faded and then died. In the churches, and in the museums, where her father, a newspaper publisher, took her, there were jewel-encrusted icons and books encased in gold and silver and pearls. In the hospitals soldiers, stuffed

three to a bed, called to Tanya in her role of volunteer nurse, "Mademoiselle, will you please just touch my hand?"

Tanya measures her life in terms of the historical events that have swept her from country to country, from life to life. Turn-of-the-century Russia. The Revolution. Japan. Germany in full-blown hysteria after World War I. France and Left Bank Paris in the frenetic days between the wars. Hitler. World War II. Flight into Spain, as Jews. America.

Bucky notches his life according to the scientific discoveries and technological advances that have made his world travels both necessary and possible. Born on July 12, 1895, in Milton, Massachusetts, he was three when radium was discovered; nine when the airplane was invented; ten when Einstein explained his theory of relativity; thirty-two when Lindbergh flew alone across the Atlantic; forty-three when the jet plane made his forty-eight trips around the world a feasibility.

There were 700 members of his class at Harvard, but only two, he remembers now, owned automobiles. And one of those was Ray Stanley, whose father had invented the Stanley Steamer. That was the class of '17. By graduation day, however, Bucky had been thrown out—"fired," he calls it—twice. The first time he was dismissed for cutting exams and squandering his tuition money on a memorable spree for the cast of the *Ziegfeld Follies;* the second for a mutually diagnosed "lack of sustained interest in the processes within the university." He was the first male member of his family since 1760 who did not graduate from Harvard.

Bucky's memories of his World War I assignments in the Navy center on his participation in the development of ship-to-plane "radiotelephony." His view of the Versailles Peace Conference—which so brutally exacerbated the war scars of Europe—is the first long-distance wireless arc telephony, which he helped install in the *USS George Washington,* the ship on which President Wilson traveled to France.

In World War I, Bucky has said, industry made the jump "from the track to the trackless, from the wire to the wireless, from visible structuring to invisible structuring of alloys." Bucky calls this "invisible" behavior of whole systems unpredictable by the individual behavior of its parts "synergy." Since World War I, advances in this realm—recently exemplified by the black box that can accommodate all of man's body functions in space—have for the first time in history made it possible to do a great deal more with infinitely less. There is enough for everyone in the world, and it is time to drop "killingry" in favor of "livingry." Now at last, at this moment of time, Bucky is sure, man has an opportunity to make a success of himself. The catch is that time is running out and the impending deadline keeps the eighty-seven-year-old technological prophet restlessly traveling, endlessly addressing anyone who will listen anywhere in the world.

There was a period from 1927 to 1929, however, when Bucky said hardly anything at all to anyone. In 1922, on her fourth birthday, his daughter Alexandra died of successive epidemics of influenza, spinal meningitis, and infantile paralysis. Bucky began drinking heavily at night, while by day he marketed a building system his father-in-law had invented. In 1927, after a takeover attempt, the business failed. The trustees blamed Bucky. After that he had nothing, including faith in people he had assumed to be his friends. Besides, his daughter Allegra had been born.

"I appeared to myself, in retrospect, a horrendous mess," Bucky once remembered, for *Quest* magazine. "I found myself saying, 'Am I an utter failure? If so, I had better get myself out of the way, so at least my wife and baby can be taken care of by my family.' "

He stood at the shore of Lake Michigan, wondering whether it might not be best for his wife and child if he threw himself in. Instead he determined to dedicate the bundle of unique experience that he was to understanding the universe. For two years he reexamined everything he had ever felt, believed, learned, read, or anything anyone had ever taught him—including the meaning of language itself—in the light of his own empirical experience.

In 1930, about a year after he had ended his self-imposed silence, Bucky succumbed to Allegra's pleas to "Tell me about Goldilocks and the Three Bears, Daddy." As the story changed and became a seminar, meandering into the lands of geometry, history, sociology, physics, chemistry, and architecture, Bucky developed what has since become his public speaking style. He approaches a subject obliquely, veers off in whatever promising direction occurs to his fertile brain, only to return once more to the point, which is a convincing tetrahedral view of the universe.

In those stories, too, he practiced his

newly evolved, idiosyncratic vocabulary, which to this day states his difficult concepts economically and with exacting accuracy. Bucky's words have the staccato sound of the machine shop to them. The way in which he sets words to work is both practical and poetic—the kind of poetry Ralph Waldo Emerson was talking about when he spoke of saying the most important things in the simplest ways. Bucky, for instance, finds Einstein's $E = MC^2$ sheer poetic beauty. The stringent richness of his language has not gone unobserved. When Bucky finally returned to Harvard in 1961, it was as Charles Eliot Norton Professor of Poetry. Such absurd twists as that caused Bucky to exclaim on the day of his Museum of Modern Art opening, "My life is proof that the impossible happens, so I pay attention to nonsense." The particular nonsense he had in mind that day was a fortune cookie that foolishly admonished him to "walk softly on new blades of grass." He is far too wholehearted for that sort of tiptoeing. He'd rather "cast myself in God's hands absolutely," he told Tanya. "God is good and God is right, even when we don't think so."

Tanya shares that mystical trust in a "meant" universe. So many terrifying, inexplicable, and marvelous things have happened to her in her life that she is a firm believer in miracles. There were the multiple miracles of the escape she and Maurice made from Nazi-occupied France in 1942, climaxed by a memorable climb over the Pyrenees into Spain. Tanya in her fur coat, Maurice with his easel. Not a toothbrush between them, they were artist and wife on a sketching expedition. When an official asked to see their papers, they showed him a certificate from the Louvre giving Maurice permission to copy in oil Velasquez' portrait of the Infanta. It worked. Tanya loved that walk across the Pyrenees. "I felt extremely in my element," she remembers of that time. "I felt beautiful. Maurice—he was more frightened at first than I was, but then he found the rhythm."

Once in New York, in 1943, Maurice painted and earned a living teaching and painting and making silk-screen reproductions, and Tanya resumed her role of *femme d'artiste*. This is how she describes that life:

"A *femme d'artiste* is a profession almost. You are everything. You are the muse, the inspiration. You hope you are until someone else walks in and takes your place. You are the participant, the audience. You share the life of the artist. It's very unpredictable, unstable. He relies on himself. You are very protective promoting him. You try to take the burden. You have great belief, great faith in a great destiny. Someday everything will be glorious and fine."

In the sweltering summer of 1944 Tanya and Maurice visited friends on Long Island and decided to find a room with kitchen privileges to rent. All the rooms they saw were both dreadful and expensive, and Maurice, for one, wanted to go home. But Tanya, feeling something "meant" about their quest, insisted on staying, on walking on a particular road that felt right. And soon a long black limousine gave them a lift, and the gentleman riding in it invited them to come back at the end of the day if they had not found anything. When they returned, there were two gentlemen—Dominican brothers, they learned later—trimming the roses outside a mansion. The dilapidated caretaker's cottage the brothers showed the couple became 5 Skidmore Place, and the rent was fifteen dollars a month. "It was," Tanya often says in the telling, "as if an angel had passed." By the time Maurice became ill in 1955, the Grosmans had bought the house, and it was there to live in while Tanya looked for something to which she could dedicate everything she had learned and felt and loved in her life—and earn money, too.

"There is a now," she says. "Today is a day, and you have to survive the day. I had to face the world and there are many ways you can face the world and the way I faced the world was my way. There are better ways to do it, but you have to have faith in life, faith in miracles, something like that."

First she tried silk-screen reproductions, but that fast-turnover technique was not suited to her ideas of perfection. And there was once again a "meant" aspect to the discovery of lithographic stones on her own doorway path in 1957. She decided to make books. Limited-edition books first; later, books for mass circulation. In the meantime she and her artists began making lithographs.

Lithographs were simply not interesting to most American artists in the 1950s. Larry Rivers was the first artist she approached. He agreed to collaborate with his friend, the poet Frank O'Hara, on what would become the lithographic portfolio *"Stones,"* only because of his relationship with Tanya, who had listened to his stories of an unhappy romance. "Among my peer group," he says, "lithography was thought to be like the work of some downtown cornball who smoked a pipe and thought of himself as a 'serious' artist." But Tanya, with her passion for ink, for the artists themselves, and for the act of creation most of all, helped change all that. What matters at ULAE is the process. She suggested that Marisol cover her body with oil and lie on two large stones for one print; that Oldenburg try painting his teapot on Balinese toilet paper; that Rauschenberg collaborate with the French novelist Alain Robbe-Grillet and the Russian poet Andrei Voznesensky. In Tanya's studio the love of creating is at once as palpable and as intangible as music.

Robert Motherwell has written of "the ambience of her workshops, where it is simply assumed that the world of the spirit exists as concretely as lemon yellow or woman's hair, but transcends everyday life.

Bucky's most famous accomplishments have occurred in a world more commonly understood as concrete. He invented the Dymaxion house in 1927; the Dymaxion three-wheeled automobile in 1932–34; the Dymaxion World Map in 1935. The ubiquitous Geodesic Dome was first built commercially in 1950. All those inventions, however, are precessional by-products of his real concern with the structure of the universe. He is thoroughly at home with intangibles, and from the first day he was completely comfortable at 5 Skidmore Place as well.

February 26, 1975, was Bucky's second day at ULAE. By then he had decided what he would do there. He would tell the story of Goldilocks as he had told it to Allegra. Through Goldilocks he would expound the theories in *Synergetics* as if he were explaining them to a child. "If I'm wrong," he said, "a child won't go for it. A child is the litmus test of the truth of a scientist." Synergetics had been, in his words, "All immaculate mathematics." *Tetrascroll* would also be feeling and fun. Its message might reach people who did not understand his other books, and Bucky felt some urgency in finishing it. "The Red Sea is still open," he kept repeating. "We have to get this book out before it closes. Humanity needs its integrity and information."

He showed Tanya his meticulously plotted itinerary for the next two years, each short stop in his round-the-world schedule studded with flight numbers, speaking engagements, hotel names and telephone numbers. ULAE was quickly insinuated into the schedule, dropping into tight crevices of time or prying less important engagements off the page. It was Tuesday when Bucky first arrived, Wednesday when he came back to work in earnest.

Once again he sat in the front room at the round table, and a lithographic stone was brought to him. On it he drew the picture of Goldilocks on the beach and the Three Bears in the heavens, which opens this book. The original text recorded his delight with the vocabulary of the stone:

"Goldy says, 'I have drawn Mommy Bear in reverse. I forgot when I was drawing her that if it is to be printed directly from my drawing, it requires an original mirror-image master. But I am going to leave her that way because it's well to remind everyone at the outset that we can only get from here to there by a series of errors . . .'"

Lithography: An artist draws an image on a large, flat, smoothed-off stone (or zinc or aluminum plate) with either a special crayon or an oily liquid called tusche. The stone is then prepared by a printer and inked. When stone and paper are run through the press, the ink adheres to the paper, leaving an image which is a mirror image of the one drawn on the stone. At ULAE artists and printers have evolved all sorts of innovative variations on this technique.

When Barnett Newman created his deluxe, limited-edition book *18 Cantos* at ULAE, the introduction he wrote became a kind of credo for lithography:

"It [lithography] is an instrument. It is not a 'medium'; it is not a poor man's substitute for painting or for drawing. Nor do I consider it to be a kind of translation of something from one medium into another. For me, it is an instrument that one plays. It is like a piano or an orchestra, and as with an instrument, it interprets. And as in all the interpretive arts, so in lithography, creation is joined with the 'playing'; in this case not of bow and string, but of stone and press. The definition of a lithograph is that it is writing on stone. But unlike Gertrude Stein's rose, the stone is not a stone. The stone is a piece of paper."

Bucky's first work session at ULAE lasted for three days and nights with brief intervals for naps. By 5:30 Sunday morning, with twelve drawings completed, Bucky felt ready to permit Bill Goldston, ULAE's studio manager, to drive him to the airport, to catch the 6:30 flight to Philadelphia. "Now, Bill," said Bucky, setting down his bags in the waiting room, "I'll be okay. You drive safely and get some sleep. After that, an exhausted

Tanya did not venture out of bed for two full days.

To Bucky, Bill Goldston—the man who gets impossible things done with ease—was "My Dear Man." To Goldston, Dr. Fuller was the much honored genius of whom he had been aware even as a boy growing up on an Oklahoma farm. At the University of Minnesota in 1970 Goldston had tried hard to get into an overflowing Buckminster Fuller lecture, and had failed. His well-informed reverence for Bucky's ideas was an integral part of the atmosphere that buoyed the work.

Early on, Bucky and the ULAE crew evolved a modus operandi that lasted throughout the nine months they worked together. While Bucky drew on his stones at one end of the long kitchen table, Tony Towle or another poet, Paul Violi, typed up the text that Bucky had scrawled in longhand on yellow sheets of paper, or white sheets, or whatever lay at hand. Freshly typed copy galvanizes Bucky, as his *Synergetics* co-participant, E. J. Applewhite, had already discovered. Bucky is moved to decorate clean copy with worms, squiggles, and inserts wedged willy-nilly into corners and between lines. In the case of *Tetrascroll* he was also dictating as he went along. There was a great deal of cutting and pasting. "Collaging," Goldston calls it. "It was a very creative process."

ULAE had no quarrel at all with Bucky's habits. Later, at a party celebrating *Tetrascroll*'s creation, he would be moved to say, "You can't go all the way to heaven and back. But you can go almost there when you go to Universal Limited Art Editions." Fostering creativity is ULAE's primary industry. So

Tanya goes to great lengths to construct a conducive setting, made up in equal parts of fine food, splendid company, a sense that time is seamless, and subtle reassurances provided by an author's books or an artist's work spread out in full view. She even dresses the part—a Russian-look blouse for the Russian poet Voznesensky; a South American coat Rauschenberg had given her when he arrives alone. All the elements must be in place, the stage set. Then the play can begin.

She has no doubt that the process of creation is one of evolution; she is quite content to patiently let matters take their course. It took six years for a prickly collaboration between Robert Rauschenberg and Alain Robbe-Grillet to produce the subtle and exquisite limited-edition book *Traces Suspectes en Surface,* nine years for Larry Rivers and Terry Southern to finish their crazy fairy tale, *The Donkey and the Darling.* At ULAE *Tetrascroll* easily expanded from its originally planned twelve pages to twenty-six. The preface page was signed on November 15, 1975, which is usually the signal that a work is complete. But Bucky drew two more stones after that. He always seemed to have more to wedge in here and there, to explicate a thought or accommodate yet another energetic drawing. That was fine. At ULAE it is assumed that the best work sometimes comes out of accidents. Once, when Rauschenberg was working there, the stone broke on the press. He tried again. It happened a second time. "Print it," he said. The print was named "Accident," and it won the Grand Prize at the International Biennial Exhibition of Prints in Ljubljana, Yugoslavia in 1963.

Bucky's staple—talk—is a primary ingredient at the long dinners in ULAE's white kitchen or during lunches outside under the catalpa tree. The artist who is working that day sits in the place of honor, at the head of the table. Friends, printers, staff, and guests range around. The food that day is the artist's favorite. The talk, that easy family-joke chatter of people who have spent satisfying hours working together. Anecdotes. Ideas.

On one particular night, when the work had been long and hard and the dinner break did not come until 8:30, Tanya pointedly instructed her husband, Maurice, not to ask any questions. Bucky's custom of answering every question from the very beginnng of time was well known by then, and everyone was very tired that night. Undaunted and irrepressible, however, Maurice asked—there must have been a gleam in his knowing eye—"Dr. Fuller, what do you think of the Mideast situation?"

Bucky lay down his knife and fork and said, "Well, at the time of the pharaohs . . ." The steak had long been forgotten when Maurice went up to bed at eleven o'clock, but Bucky was still talking to anyone else left to listen. Three hours later a new drawing was born—the one that shows Naga and Eden, and how the horizon looks like a snake's back. The talk was father to the drawing; the drawing spawned the text. The text spurred Bucky

"A pure vision expressed in lithography." — Tatyana Grosman

to try more drawings and yet more text.

At first Bucky was unsure about the drawing part. Helped by Schlossberg, who constructed models of Bucky's geometric forms, he drew the triangles for his description of cubes and his definition of the tetrahedron. The absurdly charming, pregnant lady, however, was Bucky's own roguish invention. As he worked, he grew surer of his medium. He wanted a sailor's luminous sky— and he got it. The last stone he drew—the one of a gyroscope in a cube—is shaded, complex, and beautiful. Once before, when he was technical consultant to *Fortune* magazine from 1938 to 1940, Bucky had drawn a gyroscope in order to prove that it was possible to reduce complicated concepts to forms that people could understand with their senses. This time, he feels, he did it better.

Sometimes he would make additions to a completed stone. He was accustomed to working that way with text on paper; why not with drawing on a stone? The bridge is a post-completion addition to the stone on which scissors cohabitate with a necklace. At the end of March, 1975, Bucky for the first time brought his wife, Ann, to ULAE. By then, Towle's diary entries had a frantic sound to them:

"April 2. Dr. Fuller went to New York (Thursday also) to meet with his publishers and do TV and radio interviews in connection with his new book, 'Synergetics' . . . Everyone here relaxed for two days, which was afforded by Dr. Fuller's absence." The pace accelerated. Bucky arrived at 3 P.M. on Friday, May 16, missing by a few hours the live wires that had littered the street after a storm. He declined the motel room that usually was reserved for him.

"He told Tanya not to waste her money on a Holiday Inn, as he had to take a 9 A.M. plane to San Francisco and would nap here," Towle noted in his diary. From San Francisco Saturday night Bucky would fly to Washington to talk with President Ford, and then he and Mrs. Fuller would head for a convention in Atlanta "for some fun"—was Towle's ironic comment.

Usually Bucky did sleep at the Holiday Inn, however briefly. Each morning Goldston would fetch him in the big white ULAE Olds. Bucky would be silent during the ride, but at breakfast, the sun pouring in over his left shoulder, Tanya at his right, a sleekly designed brown teapot between them, Bucky would begin to speak.

"In the car I was thinking of the Lord's Prayer," he would say. Then he would fold his hands and repeat his own version of the prayer. Each morning there was a different variation. Like every other idea he encounters Bucky has rethought the Lord's Prayer from the very beginning. Tanya was coming to feel she was participating in a religious experience.

Then, on June 23, 1975, John McKendry died. He was forty-two. As curator of the Department of Prints and Photographs at the Metropolitan Museum of Art, he had been one of Tanya's most loyal and cogent supporters. In his catalog introduction to Motherwell's *A la Pintura* McKendry had written about Tanya's "unrelenting and unreasonable love of illustrated books . . . It begins with a passion for paper . . . Like all great loves,

Tatyana's transforms its object. Like an alchemist changing lead into gold, she transforms this beautiful but simple substance into something so precious that its worth is beyond measure."

Tanya was at the hospital when McKendry died. Just minutes before, he had recognized her in his delirium, and he had spoken of building a door in his room so that she could work on the other side. "He didn't want to die," she was sure. "He wanted to work." She telephoned ULAE.

Bucky was working there that day, and she told him, "A young friend has died." "There is no death," Bucky answered. It took Tanya three years to begin talking about that telephone conversation, and she was very small, and very intense in the telling. "Dr. Fuller said, 'He is alive. There is always life in a different variation. He is alive in a different way, but we cannot communicate with him.' That consoled me."

It consoled her even more eight months later, when Maurice Grosman died, on February 12, 1976. Maurice, the very essence of adventurous, jolly life. Who had shared the bad time with her in Germany. The artists' life in France. The flight across the Pyrenees. The New York years, and ULAE. She had retreated to her bed when Bucky called. He repeated, "Maurice is close to you, but you cannot comprehend it," she remembers now. "Without my knowing him well, Buckminster Fuller was vital at these two very painful moments, like a wound. He was with me."

Bucky believes that life is synergy, not chemistry. His quite specific view of what we call death is enunciated in *Tetrascroll:*

"When human organisms are declared dead, all the physical chemistry misidentified by scientists as constituting the prime ingredients of human life are as yet present, ergo, those who speak of 'the chemistry of life' are, unwittingly, self-misinforming. Life is not physical. Life is indestructible, immortal, eternal. Life is only weightlessly and omni-invisible present."

It is all, once again, based on the tetrahedron, on the way energy ebbs and flows in the universe, how "the weightless metaphysical tetrahedron is lost and regained in the universe as life dies out here and is reborn there."

It all begins again. That is why, instead of an epilog, Schlossberg provided an "Epilever" for *Tetrascroll.* He likes to pause when he mentions it. And smile. After all, "epilever" is such a Buckminster Fuller pun. Instead of acting as an ending, the "log" is made into a lever; an epilever brings the whole experience once more around to the beginning.

The exhibit of *Tetrascroll* at the Museum of Modern Art and at Ronald Feldman Fine Arts, in January, 1977, was one beginning. Bill Goldston had been up all night helping complete the binding, on which Tanya lavished the same care she bestows on every detail. She had chosen the Dacron out of which sails are made because Bucky adored his boat *Intuition,* and because he thinks the water-sailing peoples of the world long ago discovered the earth's secrets and still best understand how to live.

At one point Tanya had considered red for the binding. She remembered that Chinese junks have reddish sails. Someone informed her the sails were dyed in pigs' blood.

"Tetrascroll is what happened in the interaction between two formidable systems named Buckminster Fuller and Tatyana Grosman."

"We spoke to Mr. Fu of the Hong Kong Tourist Bureau," Towle recorded in his diary, "who said the color of the sails is presently achieved by less exotic means."

The binding in its final form was an off-white-gray, the color of a seagull's feathers. The book had been sent out into the world. With his hectic schedule Bucky did not see it again until a February day in 1980, when he found himself with a few free hours in New York. Between dropping off his latest book at his publishers and changing into a black tie for a dinner honoring Isamu Noguchi's exhibition at the Whitney Museum, Bucky rode out to West Islip.

Once again, it was cold when Bucky arrived at ULAE. This time, however, the air was gray, with a blurred-over sun. Slightly to the east it was snowing in a half-hearted sort of way. Bucky looked over the new, facsimile version of *Tetrascroll,* enjoying the encounter. At lunch he told of his recent trip to China, the first in his life. But there was much that remained unspoken. Both Bucky and Tanya had been ill since they had seen each other last.

After naps for each, Bucky sat once more at the round white table, in his black suit and crisp blue shirt. Tanya came downstairs, all in black, wearing her grandmother's pearls and diamonds around her neck. Suddenly Bucky said, "I can't get over looking at Tatyana. She's so beautiful. The sensitivity. The loveliness."

Maurice had once used almost those same words. At the time he was looking at a photograph that Rauschenberg would eventually transform into a lithograph called "Tanya."

When Bucky said the words, Tanya glowed for a moment and lifted her chin in remembered coquetry. Then she began to cry a little. And she spoke of John McKendry and Maurice, of how Bucky had helped her when they died. And Bucky said, "I say it is a mistake for humanity to make the assumption that the thing life is what we see. Physical. We're only a transceiver—very fancy, very efficient." And then there was a silence. They looked at one another. And he chortled in his throat. And grinned his transforming grin. And Tanya said, "Dr. Fuller is a very wise man." And then, "My friend, Dr. Fuller."

"Everything I think and feel in mathematics and philosophy and everything else."

TETRASCROLL

Here is Goldy having a sky party with her three friends, the Polar Bear family. Goldy says the sky party is a "system" because Goldy plus the Three Bears equals four entities (or star events), and it takes four events to produce a system. A system divides all the universe into six parts: all the universe outside the system (the macrocosm), all the universe inside the system (the microcosm), and the four star events *A, B, C, D,* which do the dividing.

The tetrahedron's four-corner star events do not have to occur at the same time. Goldy found that light traveled six and one-half trillion miles in a year, and was fascinated when an astronomer told her that the star in the nose of the Big Bear is a live show taking place 210 light-years away-and-ago, as the American colonists are first thinking about revolting from English rule: and the pole star at Mommy Bear's nose is a live show taking place 680 light-years away-and-ago, as Dante is writing *The Inferno:* and the star at Wee Bear's front toe is a live show taking place forty-three light-years away-and-ago as Franklin Delano Roosevelt is being elected to the USA presidency for the first time, at the depth of the great 1929–39 Depression: While she, Goldy, is also a live show taking place no time away-and-ago. Altogether Goldy's four live shows constitute a scenario of nonsimultaneous but omni-interrelated events, which can and do define the four corners of a minimum system—the tetrahedron.

She now understands Einstein's concept that Universe is a scenario and not a single simultaneous structure. One picture of a caterpillar does not tell you it is going to transform into a butterfly, and it takes many frames of the cinema to inform you that the butterfly can fly.

STONE 1

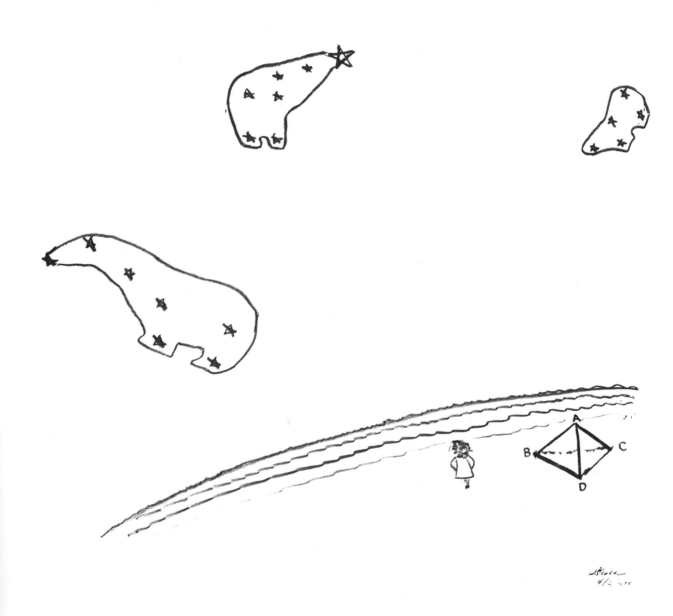

Here is Goldy having a sky party with her three friends, the Polar Bear family. Big Bear gave Mommy the Pole Star to wear on her nose when she gave birth to

EE BEAR.

Daddy—Ursa Major, "The Big Bear"—is often called the "Big Dipper" because he drinks so much iced tea. Mommy—Ursa Minor, "The Little Bear"—is usually called the "Little Dipper" because being right at the cold North Pole she drinks much hot tea but in little cups—that way it doesn't have time to get cold, she says. Wee Bear is sometimes called Cassiopeia because he sits in the high chair Cassiopeia used when she was a baby.

Goldy says, "I have drawn Mommy Bear in reverse. I forgot when I was drawing her that if it is to be printed directly from my drawing, it requires an original mirror-image master. But I am going to leave her that way because it's well to remind everyone at the outset that we can only get from here to there by a series of errors—errors forwardly to the right, then a correcting forwardly error to the left, each time reducing error but never eliminating it. This is what generates waves; this what generates the experience life."

Goldy says the sky is a "system" because Goldy plus the Three Bears equals four entities (or star events), and it takes four events to produce a system. A system divides all the universe into six parts: all the universe outside the system (the macrocosm), all the universe inside the system (the microcosm), and the four star events *A, B, C, D,* which do the dividing.

Two star or three star event-entities have only "Betweenness" but no "insideness."

Insideness outsideness separation begins only with completion of the six interrelationship lines of the four separate entity-producing events. The four star events *A, B, C, D,* have six separate,

4

unique and most economical interrelationship lines *AB, AC, AD, BC, BD, CD*. These six lines and their four interconnected star-corners inadvertently produce four triangular facets of the minimum polyhedron—which four facets completely enclose the system to exclude the macrocosm and include the microcosm. A system consists at minimum of four nonsimultaneous but co-occurrent, because overlapping, yet dissimilarly beginning and enduring star entity-events of six interrelationship lines and four nothingness-window-facets plus twelve unique intercovariant vertex angles—twenty-six conceptual, topological components of a system to which must be added the multiplicative, ultravisible, macrocosmic outsideness and infravisible, microcosmic insideness as well as the inseparably co-occurring inside concavity and outside convexity and the bipoled axis of rotation of all systems: for a total component inventory of thirty-two items.

Three thousand years ago the Greek geometers named this minimum system the tetrahedron—tetra = four, hedron = sides.

A system cannot have less than four triangular polygon "faces" (or sides or windows) or less than three triangular (polygon) faces surrounding each of the system's four event corners. The triangle is the minimum polygon face. You cannot have a polygon of less than three edges. You cannot have a location fix-point that is less than one fix-point, you cannot have an event tracing line that is less than a line, you cannot have an angle that is less than a minimum angle, and you cannot have a system of less than thirty-two uniquely differentiable and geometrically describable characteristics. All the characteristics of a system are absolute because each of its components is the minimum-limit case in its respective conceptual category, for all conceptuality, as the great mathematican Euler discovered and proved, consists at minimum of points, areas, and lines. Goldy further clarifies and simplifies Euler by saying an area is nothingness, a plurality of areas are framingly separated views of nothingness, a point is a somethingness. A line is a relationship between two somethingnesses. An enlarged, seemingly single somethingness may prove to consist of a plurality of somethingnesses between which the defined interrelationship lines fence off the nothingness into a plurality of separate views of the same nothingnesses. Points are unresolvable, untunable somethingness occurring in the twilight zone between visible and subvisible. Nothingness is the unresolvable untunableness occurring in the twilight zone between visible and supravisible experience.

Life minimally described is "awareness," which is inherently plural, for at minimum it consists of the individual system which becomes aware and the first minimum "otherness" of which it is aware, the otherness being either integrally internal or separately external to the observing system's fourteen integral, topologically componented subsystems ($4V + 4A + 6L$).

Together the observer and the observed constitute two points differentiated against an omni-environment of nothingness with one inherent line of "awareness" interrelationship running between these two points. Euler's generalized formula, which he named topology, says the number of points plus the number of areas will always equal the number of lines plus the number 2, which Goldy finds to be at minimum $2P + 1A = 1L + 2$, which minimum set of awareness aspects of life adds to four, i.e., (A) the observer, (B) the observed, (C) the line of interrelationship, and (D) the nothingness area against which the somethingness is observed.

There are no known experimentally demonstrable absolute maximum limits.

Only the minimum limit is demonstrably absolute. The minimum limit experienceible is always a system—even when it looks only like a point. A point is a system so macro remote or micro small as to appear only as an indivisible something in a specific direction relationship to the observer's integral systems arrangement of, for instance, head, toe, front, and back. "That's nifty," says Wee Bear. "It's magnificent," says Big Bear. "I call it both nifty and magnificent," says Mommy Bear.

Goldy has a tetrahedron beside her on the beach. Its four vertexes (which may also be called: locations; stars, event-fixes; points) are oriented as are Goldy and the Three Bears, with Mommy and her pole star at A, Daddy at B, Wee Bear at C, and Goldy at D.

The tetrahedron's four-corner star events do not have to occur at the same time. Goldy saw a man way down the beach pounding to drive a post into the sand. She heard each pounding a moment after she saw it occur. When she was told about light's speed having been measured in a vacuum by scientists, she understood that the light with which she saw the event, like sound, also had a limit speed. She was told that sound traveled at about 700 miles an hour and that light traveled a million times faster, which though very fast is much slower than 700 million miles in no time at all.

Multiplying 700 million by the number of hours in a year, Goldy found that light traveled six and one-half trillion miles in a year, and was fascinated when an astronomer told her that the star in the nose of the Big Bear is a live show taking place 210 light-years away-and-ago, as the American colonists are first thinking about revolting from English rule: and the pole star at Mommy Bear's nose is a live show taking place 680 light-years away-and-ago, as Dante is writing *The Inferno:* and the star at Wee Bear's front toe is a live show taking place forty-three light-years away-and-ago as Franklin Delano Roosevelt is being elected to the USA presidency for the first time, at the depth of the great 1929–39 Depression: while she, Goldy, is also a live show taking place no time away-and-ago. Altogether Goldy's four live shows constitute a scenario of nonsimultaneous but omni-interrelated events, which can and do define the four corners of a minimum system—the tetrahedron. Goldy, too, is a nonsimultaneous system. She, too, is a nonsimultaneous and only partially overlapping complex of insideness and outsideness experiences. The interrelated experiences of Goldy and the Three Bears are a scenario. She now understands Einstein's concept that Universe is a scenario and not a single simultaneous structure. One picture of a caterpillar does not tell you it is going to transform into a butterfly, and it takes many frames of the cinema to inform you that the butterfly can fly and many thousands of frames to permit a possible replicative engineering discovery of how it can fly. Because of any one single "frame" or picture in the scenario filmstrip cannot disclose "what the story is all about," Goldy says to the bears, "When people look at you stars and say, 'I wonder what is outside the outside of the stars,' they are asking for a timeless, simultaneous, static-system concept where none exists. Their question is as ignorant as would be asking, 'Which word is the dictionary?' "

"You are right, Goldy," says Daddy Bear. "Minds think exploratorially, sort and compose. One thought, which is one metaphysically conceptual system, which at minimum is one tetrahedron, can interrelate any four event points or subsystems in nonsimultaneous Universe. Because of inherent nonsimultaneity all thinking is tetratuning. The (system-thought) tetrahedron can and always does include four identities: (1) the thinking individual, (2) the present otherness, (3) the past otherness, (4) the future otherness.

To which thought of Daddy Bear Mommy adds, "And the ignorant question asking of the brain occurs because brains do not think. They only play back yesterday's recordings. Brains are pretuned like bells and sound off when struck."

TRICAP 2

Using the vast, water-smoothed surface of the many-miles-long sandy beach, and walking along as she talks, Goldy keeps drawing pictures large enough for the bears to see. Goldy says to the bears, "Let's try an experiment with our tetrahedron."

By pushing successively on the tetrahedron's top vertex, Goldy keeps rolling the tetrahedron ahead of her across the beach. This succession of rollings makes a long, parallel-edged ribbon with a line zigzagging between its edges to produce a succession of adjacent triangles.

Goldy says to the bears, "We have discovered a triangularly subdivided ribbon-printing machine—a wave-printing machine." And Daddy Bear says, "That is also the sand print patterning made by our four (A, B, C, D) bear's feet when we are running. We can start our run with our right hind foot D elevated. We then lunge forwardly over the hinge line running between our two front feet $C, D,$ as foot A goes forwardly and down while foot B is elevated. Because a bear's foot is itself a triangle, Goldy makes a pattern of Big Sky Bear's footprints as he walks or runs eastwardly along the beach. Goldy uses the successive triangles as the frames for the succession of illustrations of her conversation with the bears. She says the ribbon is like a scenario filmstrip with the successive triangular pictures overlapping instead of being vertically separated.

STONE 2

Using the vast, water-smoothed surface of the many-miles-long sandy beach, and walking along as she talks, Goldy keeps drawing pictures large enough for the bears to see. The pictures illustrate each of her experimentally demonstrated explanations. She is recounting to the bears what humans have thus far learned regarding the principles employed by Scenario Universe to accomplish its eternal regeneration.

Goldy says to the bears, "Let's try an experiment with our tetrahedron. Let's see what happens if I use three of its four corners, *A*, *B*, *C*, representing you three bears, as the tetrahedron's base on the sand—because you have been together for billions of years—and corner *D*, which is the newcomer me—Goldy—I put at the top of the tetrahedron. Now I am taking hold of my corner *D* at the top and am rolling it over around its bottom edge *BC* until corner *D* lies down in the sand, pointing in an easterly direction to my right, along the beach." This rolling leaves the triangular print *ABC* in the sand westward, to Goldy's left, where the tetrahedron had been sitting before that first rollover. Goldy now takes hold of corner *A*, which rose from the sand base to replace *D* at the tetrahedron's top. She pushes the new top corner *A* again over and downwardly to her right around edge *CD*, which means farther eastwardly along the beach until *A* hits the beach, as corner *B* rises to take the top corner place of the tetrahedron, leaving a second triangular print *BCD* in the sand with its edge *BC* congruent with *BC* of the first printed triangle *ABC*. She now pushes top corner *B* eastward, rolling it over and down around bottom edge *DA*, which brings corner *C* to the top and leaves a third successive triangular print *CDA*. She next rolls top corner *C* eastward over bottom edge *BA* to leave a fourth successive print *DAB*, making an altogether eastwardly developing ribbon of triangular prints. Goldy then pushes top corner *D*, then successively tops *A*, *B*, *C*, *D* again and again, as each rotates to the top to replace the one Goldy last rolled over and downward, eastwardly to her right. By pushing successively eastward the tetrahedron's successively latest top vertex, Goldy keeps rolling the tetrahedron ahead of her along the beach. This succession of rollings makes a long parallel-edged ribbon with a line zigzagging between its edges to produce a succession of adjacent triangles. One of the ribbon's edges reads successively *AC, AC, AC, AC*, while its other edge reads *BD, BD, BD, BD*. The succession of eastwardly occurring tops reads *D, A, B, C, D, A, B, C, D,* and so on.

Goldy says to the bears, "We have discovered a triangularly subdivided ribbon-printing machine—a wave-printing machine." And Daddy Bear says, "That is also the sand print patterning made by our four (*A, B, C, D*) bear's feet when we are running. We can start our run with our right hind foot *D* elevated. We then lunge forwardly over the hinge line running between our two front feet *C, D*, as foot *A* goes forwardly and down while foot *B* is elevated."

Because a bear's foot is itself a triangle, Goldy makes a pattern of Big Sky Bear's footprints as he walks or runs eastwardly along the beach. Goldy uses the successive triangles as the frames for the succession of illustrations of her conversation with the bears. She says the ribbon is like a scenario filmstrip with the successive triangular pictures overlapping instead of being vertically separated. "You may notice," says Wee Bear, "That the starry pattern of the chair Cassiopeia left for me looks like the first three triangular frames of that scenario filmstrip." "Yes," Goldy replies, "and I see that if I print these triangular frames of the scenario strip of overlapping conceptual events on a heavy paper ribbon, the strip can be spooled onto a tetrahedron. This will make a tetrahedron book that can be progressively unrolled from a tetrahedron at one end and rerolled to form another tetrahedron at the other end of the strip, with the progressively exposed strip in between telling the picture story—the scenario—of "nonsimultaneous universe," with both the four-dimensional tetrahedronal othernesses scrolls of tomorrow and yesterday as yet unrolled or already rolled back in, and therefore consciously and directionally identifiable but inscrutable. Because the tetrahedra are serving as four-dimensional scrolls, we will call our first such book *The 4D Tetrascroll.*

Goldy explains to the Three Bears that synergy means behavior of whole systems unpredicted by the behavior of any of the system's parts when each is considered only by itself. Goldy takes three triangles and brings them together edge-to-edge around a single corner and inadvertently produces the fourth base triangle. Thus she discovers that one-plus-one-plus-one equals four.

Goldy says her mommy is a system and so is her daddy. They both have insides and outsides. Goldy says parents are synergetic: 1 system + 1 system = 3 systems. One outsider plus one insider produces an additional inside-outer—Goldy.

Goldy says to the Three Bears, "If you don't understand any of my words, you can find them in the dictionary." Wee bear replies, "Out here we use cosmic thought communication. We don't have to find words in special-language diction-aries. We use a cosmic thinktionary. All your dictionaries express the universal concepts of our thinktionary but only in special, ethnic-language, sound words. The concepts such as mountain or star or nuance are the same experience engendered concepts in all languages. We understand you perfectly, Goldy."

Concepts are always synergetic systems. Systems are minimum-maximum sets of thinkable, conceptual, omni-interrelevant experience recollections, intertunably differentiated only by time out of nonsimultaneous, unitarily nonconceptual Scenario Universe.

STONE 3

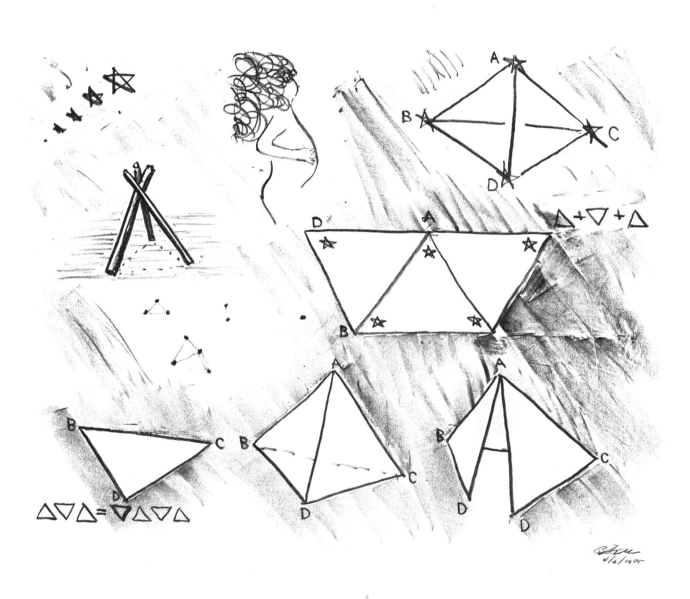

$\triangle + \nabla + \triangle$

$\triangle \nabla \triangle = \nabla \triangle \nabla \triangle$

13

Goldy explains to the Three Bears that synergy means behavior of whole systems unpredicted by the behavior of any of the system's parts when each is considered only by itself. Goldy takes three triangles and brings them together edge-to-edge around a single corner and inadvertently produces the fourth base triangle. Thus she discovers that one-plus-one-plus-one equals four. She points out that Wee Bear's three-triangle strip constellation (Cassiopeia) can be folded in the same way by bringing E to E to produce the tetrahedron. She says, "Wee Bear, by joining your end edges you can capture your own fourth invisible triangle and become a tetrahedron. You are a system. You are synergetic." She finds that synergy keeps reappearing in systems. None of the four star corners of the tetrahedron by itself suggests that the tetrahedron will have six individually unique, most economical interrelationship edges.

Goldy now sees that gravity makes the three legs of the tripod spread apart, but gravity also pulls the tripod toward the earth and also coheres the earth on which the tripod stands and gratuitously provides three more base edge lines formed as a closed tension triangle which keeps the three disintegrating tripod legs from coming apart and thus guarantees the structural integrity of the tetrahedron so formed.

Since each of the tripod's three legs is trying to part from the others, they are trying to subtract themselves from one another so they are minus quantities. Therefore, in this particular synergetic formulation's formula, one vector leg minus a second vector leg minus a third vector leg equals (results in) the six positive vector legs (3–3 = +6), which is the minimum number of structural members of a structural system.

Goldy says her mommy is a system and so is her daddy. They both have insides and outsides. Goldy says parents are synergetic: 1 system + 1 system = 3 systems. One outsider plus one insider produces an additional inside-outer—Goldy.

Goldy says to the Three Bears, "If you don't understand any of my words, you can find them in the dictionary." Wee Bear replies, "Out here we use cosmic thought communication. We don't have to find words in special-language diction-aries. We use a cosmic thinktionary. All your dictionaries express the universal concepts of our thinktionary but only in special, ethnic-language, sound words. The concepts such as mountain or star or nuance are the same experience-engendered concepts in all languages. We understand you perfectly, Goldy."

Concepts are always synergetic systems. Systems are minimum-maximum sets of thinkable, conceptual, omni-interrelevant experience recollections, intertunably differentiated only by time out of nonsimultaneous, unitarily nonconceptual Scenario Universe.

TRICAP 4

Exploring synergy further, Goldy takes apart the four edge-bonded triangles of the tetrahedron and reassociates them, this time joining them only by their vertexes, which produces the octahedron, or eight-triangular-faceted polyhedron with four inadvertently produced, structurally stable, empty triangular window facets. Here is synergy again with $1 + 1 + 1 + 1 = 8$. This clearly seen structural system's symmetrical intertransformation from 4 to 8—i.e., 1 to 2—Goldy explains, is the simple principle which, being nongeometrically conceptualized by the physicists, is called by them "a quantum leap." The scientists continue to "fly blindly on instruments." In addition to the eight triangular facets the octahedron has six vertex (star-entity) events and twelve structural edges.

Since half the triangles are empty and only half are filled, Goldy becomes curious and cuts four triangular windows in each of the four filled triangular facets, and she finds the octahedron as yet stable. It seems to Goldy that the twelve edges held together by the six vertexes must be producing the structural stability.

So Goldy next takes two sets, each of twelve equal-length tubes, threads a string through the tubes, and fastens them together in two different ways: (1) with four tubes joined at each of six corners to make the octahedron, which is structurally stable, and (2) with three tubes joined at each of eight corners to make the cube, which proves to be structurally unstable and collapses.

STONE 4

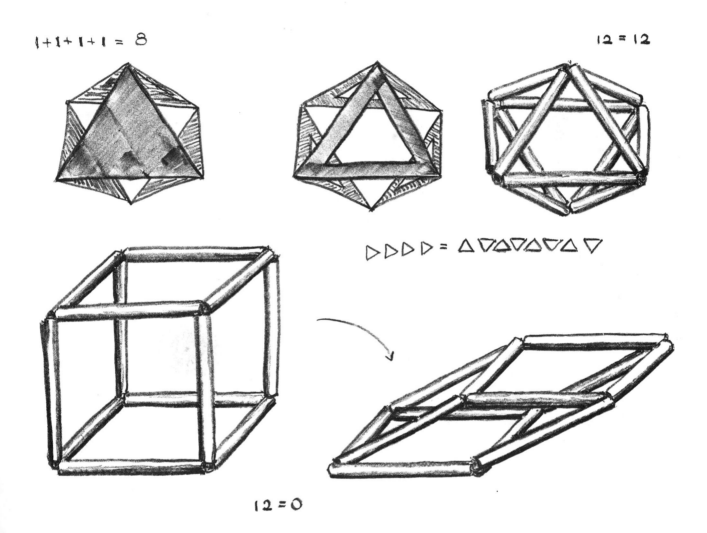

$1+1+1+1 = 8$

$12 = 12$

$\triangleright\triangleright\triangleright\triangleright = \triangle\triangledown\triangle\triangledown\triangle\triangledown\triangle\triangledown$

$12 = 0$

Exploring synergy further, Goldy takes apart the four edge-bonded triangles of the tetrahedron and reassociates them, this time joining them only by their vertexes, which produces the octahedron, or eight-triangular-faceted polyhedron with four inadvertently produced, structurally stable, empty triangular window facets. Here is synergy again with $1 + 1 + 1 + 1 = 8$. This clearly seen structural system's symmetrical intertransformation from 4 to 8—(i.e., 1 to 2)—Goldy explains, is the simple principle which, being nongeometrically conceptualized by the physicists, is called by them "a quantum leap." The scientists continue to "fly blindly on instruments." In addition to the eight triangular facets the octahedron has six vertex (star-entity) events and twelve structural edges.

Since half the triangles are empty and only half are filled, Goldy becomes curious and cuts four triangular windows in each of the four filled triangular facets, and she finds the octahedron as yet stable. It seems to Goldy that the twelve edges held together by the six vertexes must be producing the structural stability.

So Goldy next takes two sets, each of twelve equal-length tubes, threads a string through the tubes, and fastens them together in two different ways: (1) with four tubes joined at each of six corners to make the octahedron, which is structurally stable; and (2) with three tubes joined at each of eight corners to make the cube, which proves to be structurally unstable and collapses.

This brings Goldy to her necklace experiment, to discover, if possible, what produces structural stability. When the necklace flexes, the tubular beads do not bend or change their lengths. It is the tension connector angles between the tubes that change and accommodate variable draping of the necklace. One by one Goldy takes the inflexible tubes out of the necklace, which keeps on flexing around her neck and draping over her shoulders until there remain only three push-pull tubes and three tension connector angles. Now for the first time the necklace does not flex or drape around her neck. It is rigid. It is in the form of the triangle, which is the minimum polygon. There is no polygon of two sides and two angles. The necklace triangle has six separate parts: three rigid, push-pull tubular sides and three flexible tension angles, all six of which separate entity-events are interacting to produce a stable pattern. How do they do so?

Any two sides of the triangle constitute a pair of levers fulcrumed tensively together at one end—like a pair of scissors. The longer the two lever arms, the more powerful the shears. So the third side of the triangle is a rigid, push-pull strut taking hold of the two adjacent lever arms at their maximum lever-advantage ends, thereby stabilizing the angle opposite with minimum effort. So does each side of the triangle most effortlessly stabilize its opposite angle. Since a structure is a pattern-stabilizing complex of events, a triangle is structure. Structure is triangle. There are no other such minimum-effort, six-foldedly combined, minimum-limit-of-a-series, cosmic cases such as this one.

STONE 5

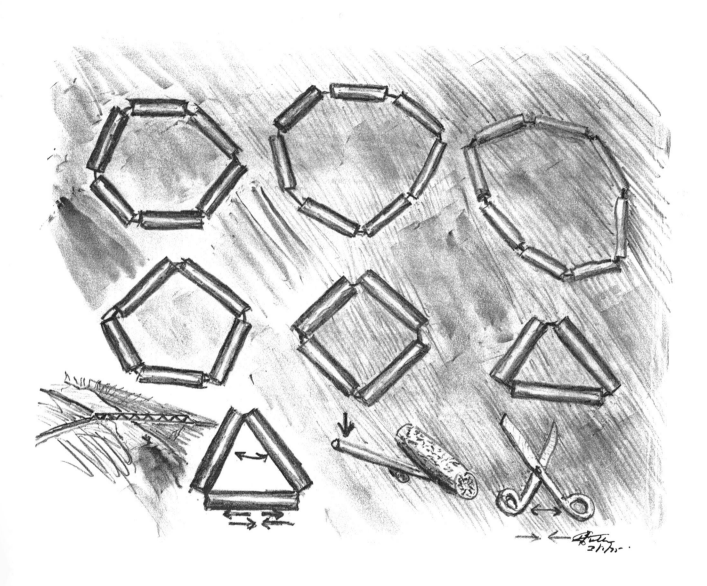

This brings Goldy to her necklace experiment, to discover, if possible, what produces structural stability. When the necklace flexes, the tubular beads do not bend or change their lengths. It is the tension connector angles between the tubes that change and accommodate variable draping of the necklace. One by one Goldy takes the inflexible tubes out of the necklace, which keeps on flexing around her neck and draping over her shoulders until there remain only three push-pull tubes and three tension connector angles. Now for the first time the necklace does not flex or drape around her neck. It is rigid. It is in the form of the triangle, which is the minimum polygon. There is no polygon of two sides and two angles. The necklace triangle has six separate parts: three rigid, push-pull tubular sides and three flexible tension angles, all six of which separate entity-events are interacting to produce a stable pattern. How do they do so?

Any two sides of the triangle constitute a pair of levers fulcrumed tensively together at one end—like a pair of scissors. The longer the two lever arms, the more powerful the shears. So the third side of the triangle is a rigid, push-pull strut taking hold of the two adjacent lever arms at their maximum lever-advantage ends, thereby stabilizing the angle opposite with minimum effort. So does each side of the triangle most effortlessly stabilize its opposite angle. Since a structure is a pattern-stabilizing complex of events, a triangle is structure. Structure is triangle. There are no other such minimum-effort, six-foldedly combined, minimum-limit-of-a-series, cosmic cases such as this one, which integrates: (1) minimum effort, (2) minimum system, (3) minimum polygon, (4) minimum polyhedron, (5) minimum conceptuality, (6) minimum thinkaboutedness, all resulting in complex self-interstabilization. All six of these minimum-limit conditions in an hierarchical series of conceptualities are utterly independent of size and time. So the tetrahedron, consisting exclusively of triangles, is not only the minimum system in Universe but is also the minimum structural system in Universe. It is the initiating point of the awareness which we call life. No otherness, no awareness. The minimum otherness is the minumum structural system in Universe—the tetrahedron—the minimum conceptuality—the minimum thought.

Goldy says to the bears, "Since the minimum otherness may look like a 'speck' but, when magnified, always proves to be a system or a complex of systems, there is no experienceable "one, two, or three dimensionality." Dimensionality is at minimum four. All experience begins with a tetrahedronal system or a complex tetrahedronal structure, and all tetrahedra are four-dimensional—that is, they have four planes of persistent symmetry." We learn of that persistent symmetry by using cheese to make (1) a cube, (2) an octahedron, (3) a dodecahedron, (4) a tetrahedron. Next we slice off a piece of cheese parallel to one of the faces of the cube—what is left is no longer a cube. If we slice parallel to one face of an octahedron, the octahedron is no longer an octahedron. So, too, is the dodecahedron destroyed by this assymetrical alteration of only one of the faces. There is, however, one exception. We slice parallel to one of the tetrahedron's faces, and what remains is a smaller but omni-symmetrical tetrahedron. We try slicing parallel to each of the tetrahedron's four faces, and what remains is always a regular tetrahedron.

TRICAP 6

In nonsimultaneous Scenario Universe every event action has both reaction and resultant "side effects" (precessions), which may be graphically represented by three angularly associated vectors that can take either open or closed forms.

The atomic proton and neutron are unique, always and only co-occurring, prime energy events of Universe. They have different mass but may be co-intertransformed by means of their two different actions and the latter's, two each, different energy "side effects." The proton and the neutron are both actions, and each has its respectively different reaction and resultant "side effects." Each of these two, three-vector teams equals one-half of an energy quantum (or one half-spin).

Because it consists of two such half-quanta of energy, the vector-edged tetrahedron exactly equals one quantum of energy and is also one minimal structural system of Universe. The six-vector tetrahedron is also synergetic in that two vector triangles combine to make the four triangles of the tetrahedron. This is not magic. The two additional invisible triangles that become visible by associating the visible pair are always secreted in the invisible complementarity reserves of the 99.9 percent invisible Universe of utterly abstract weightless principles. Employing vectors, the two convergent sides of any given angle can only be considered as potentially realizable by a third and invisible vector which invisibly holds apart the outer ends of the angle describing convergent vectors.

STONE 6

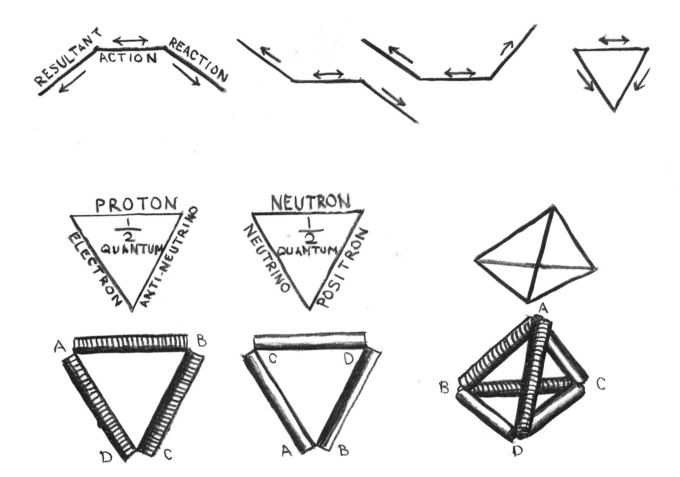

In nonsimultaneous Scenario Universe every event action has both reaction and resultant "side effects" (precessions), which may be graphically represented by three angularly associated vectors that can take either of these open or closed forms:

1 triangle + 1 triangle = 4 triangles

The atomic proton and neutron are unique, always and only co-occurring, prime energy events of Universe. They have different mass but may be co-intertransformed by means of their two different actions and the latter's, two each, different energy "side effects." The proton and the neutron are both actions, and each has its respectively different reaction and resultant "side effects." Each of these two, three-vector teams equals one-half of an energy quantum (or one half-spin).

Because it consists of two such half-quanta of energy, the vector-edged tetrahedron exactly equals one quantum of energy and is also one minimal structural system of Universe. The six-vector tetrahedron is also synergetic in that two vector triangles combined to make the four triangles of the tetrahedron. This is not magic. The two additional invisible triangles that become visible by associating the visible pair are always secreted in the invisible complementarity reserves of the 99.9 percent invisible Universe of utterly abstract weightless principles. Employing vectors, the two convergent sides of any given angle can only be considered as potentially realizable by a third and invisible vector which invisibly holds apart the outer ends of the angle describing convergent vectors. This is metaphysics and not magic. The physicist says that all the physical universe is energy—energy associative as matter and energy disassociative as radiation, both interconvertible to the other. The physicist says that the physical will always move a levered needle, either by gravity of electromagnetism. Metaphysics embraces all experiences, such as the phenomenon "understanding," which does not move a pivoted needle. The invisible metaphysical universe of pure principles complements the physical components to realize in pure abstract principle the empty yet structurally stabilizing invisible triangles.

Next Goldy says to the Three Bears, "Unlike you constellations of stars who intercoordinate with combined gravity and precession and know the most about both, few people gravitationally cohered around precessionally steered planet earth comprehend either gravity or precession."

Goldy takes a closed cylinder made of flexible rubber which is filled with water. She presses its ends toward one another, and the cylinder bulges outward radially at its mid-girth, tensively stretching the rubber outward radially in a plane perpendicular to the axis of Goldy's compressing. Next she pulls the two ends of the cylinder away from one another, and the cylinder contracts radially at its mid-girth, becoming compressed in a plane perpendicular to the axis of Goldy's pulling.

These right-angle results of applied effort are called precession. Precession is the integrated effect of bodies in motion on other bodies in motion. The gravitational interattraction of the sun and earth results in the earth traveling around the sun in an orbit perpendicular to the line of the sun's and the earth's gravitational interattraction.

Precession is regenerative. Goldy drops a stone into the water. A circular wave is generated, growing outwardly in a plane perpendicular to the axis of the stone's line of fall. Then the outward motion of the wave precesses the surrounding water, causing the water to rise as a complete circular ridge in an upward direction perpendicular to the plane of the wave's horizontally outward growth, and the rising water in turn immediately reprecesses the surrounding water into further outwardly radiating horizontal growth.

STONE 7

Next Goldy says to the Three Bears, "Unlike you constellations of stars who intercoordinate with combined gravity and precession and know the most about both, few people gravitationally cohered around precessionally steered planet earth comprehend gravity or precession."

Goldy takes a closed cylinder made of flexible rubber which is filled with water. She presses its ends toward one another, and the cylinder bulges outward radially at its mid-girth, tensively stretching the rubber outward radially in a plane perpendicular to the axis of Goldy's compressing. Next she pulls the two ends of the cylinder away from one another, and the cylinder contracts radially at its mid-girth, becoming compressed in a plane perpendicular to the axis of Goldy's pulling.

These right-angle results of applied effort are called precession. Precession is the integrated effect of bodies in motion on other bodies in motion. The gravitational interattraction of the sun and earth results in the earth traveling around the sun in an orbit perpendicular to the line of the sun's and the earth's gravitational interattraction. Thus also is the moon precessed into orbit around the earth and the electrons into orbit around their atomic nuclei. And Goldy notes that humans also are precessed into orbits around other humans with whom they share mutual interattractions. Goldy may have made the first discovery of a scientific generalization that applies to social behaviors as well as to physics.

Precession is regenerative. Goldy drops a stone into the water. A circular wave is generated, growing outwardly in a plane perpendicular to the axis of the stone's line of fall. Then the outward motion of the wave precesses the surrounding water, causing the water to rise as a complete circular ridge in an upward direction perpendicular to the plane of the wave's horizontally outward growth, and the rising water in turn immediately reprecesses the surrounding water into further outwardly radiating horizontal growth, which immediately results in a further ninety-degree change of the water molecules displacement wherein the molecules sink perpendicularly, which developing action precesses again at ninety degrees to produce further, horizontally circular, outward growth of the water wave. Thus the circularly growing waves in water are progressively precessed into their familiar but usually unexplained behaviors.

Goldy points an iron bar magnet toward the center of a coil of copper wire looped in a plane perpendicular to the axis of her bar magnet. The coil has no electrical current but is attached to an instrument that will show the presence of electricity should it develop. Always pointing with the bar magnet toward the center of the copper coil, Goldy moves the bar toward that center of the coil. An electrical current is precessionally induced in the coil, which articulates as a clockwise orbital circuit in the plane of the copper wire coil. It is to be remembered that the plane is perpendicular to the line of approach of the magnet. Instantly the electrical current reprecesses at ninety degrees to produce a positive electromagnetic force-field that opposes the magnet's approach, and the faster the magnet approaches perpendicularly to the coil, the more powerfully does the field resist it. The electrical current and its resultant force-field which opposes the approach are generated only while Goldy keeps moving the magnet perpendicularly toward the center of the copper wire coil. The instant Goldy stops moving the magnet, the complex regeneration ceases, and both the electric current and the electromagnetic field vanish. When, however, Goldy starts to withdraw the bar magnet (perpendicularly away from the center of the coil), a reverse orbital direction of the electric current is precessionally induced in the coil, which in turn precesses to produce a negative electromagnetic field that resists the magnet's further withdrawal. The faster the withdrawal, the more precessionally powerful is the field's resistance.

Thinking about precession Goldy observes that fish fan their tails sideways to produce forward motion, that snakes wriggle sideways to produce forward motion. She sees that iceboats attain speeds of sixty miles per hour in a direction at right angles to wind blowing at half that speed. Coming back to her triangles and their synergetic surprise behaviors, Goldy flips one simple white triangle over and finds the other side is black. She realizes that there are two triangles, the obverse and reverse, always and only coexisting congruently. Goldy realizes that every sphere has a concave inside and a convex outside. She knows that convex and concave are not the same because concave reflectors concentrate energy as radiation and convex mirrors diffuse the radiant energy. Convex and concave are nature's macro-to-micro or micro-to-macro radiant-energy transformers. Goldy realizes that unity is always plural and at minimum two. Unity does not mean the number one. She realizes that one does not and cannot exist by itself. In Universe life's existence begins with awareness. No otherness, no awareness. The observed requires an observer. The subjective and objective always and only coexist and therewith demonstrate the inherent plurality of unity—inseparable union. Physics tends to think of "complementarity" (discovered a half-century ago) and the latter's non-mirror-imaged complementation (discovered only 20 years ago) as being the interrelationship characteristics of two separate entities. However, the always-and-only-coexistent, non-mirror-imaged complementations also may coexist within inseparable plural unity.

Goldy finds she can interconnect the three mid-edge points of a triangle that subdivide the big triangle into four similar smaller triangles and can fold the three corner triangles along their connecting lines to produce two different tetrahedra, because folding the corner triangles under or over produces either a white tetrahedron with a black inside or a black tetrahedron with a white inside. Since the inside of the tetrahedron is concave and the outside is convex, there are two very real and separate tetrahedra in evidence whose eight (four white, four black) faces have been evolved from only four externally viewable triangles, which four were in turn evolved from one (unity is plural) triangle.

Since both the positive and negative concave tetrahedra have four different black faces and four different white faces, she can differentiate them by placing a red, a green, a yellow, and a blue dot in the center of each of their respective four white inside faces and an orange, a purple, a brown, and a gray dot in the center of each of their outside black triangles successively. Since each of the two tetrahedra can turn themselves inside out (as their respective three triangular corners or rotate around the central triangle's three edge hinges, thus to open like a three-petalled flowerbud), each tetrahedron can be opened in four such flowerbud ways with three triangular petals around each of their four respective triangular, flower-receptacle base faces. These four separate cases of inside-outing transformability permit the production of four separate and unique positive and four separate and unique negative tetrahedra, all generated from the same unity—each of which tetrahedra can rank as Nature's simplest structural system. Therefore, each prime structural system in Universe has nine separate and unique states of existence—four positive, four negative, plus one schematic unfolded nothingness state—which Goldy reminds the bears constitutes the same schematic "game" setup as that of physics quantum mechanics, with four positive and four negative "quanta" as we go from a central nothingness equilibrium to first one, then two, then three, then four high-frequency-regenerated, alternate, equi-integrity tetrahedral quanta, all eight of which have eight invisible counterparts.

	4 white, 3 petalled flowers	
	one with—red	
	one with—green	
	one with—yellow	Base
	one with—blue	receptacle

Visibly
Demonstrable
(Physical)

	4 black, 3 petalled flowers	
	one with—orange	
	one with—purple	
	one with—brown	Base
	one with—gray	receptacle

	4 white, 3 petalled flowers	
	one with—orange	
	one with—purple	
	one with—brown	Base
	one with—gray	receptacle

Invisible But
Thinkable
(Metaphysical)

	4 black, 3 petalled flowers	
	one with—red	
	one with—green	
	one with—yellow	Base
	one with—blue	receptacle

Goldy now takes any two of these triangularly petalled tetrahedra each with three sixty-degree folded corners partially open and pointing out from their bases like petals of an opening tulip bud. Goldy rotates one of the sixty-degree petalled tetrahedra a sixth of a circle turn and precesses it axially sixty degrees which points its opened triangular petals toward the other's sixty-degree openings. Goldy brings them convergently together edge-to-edge to produce the octahedron. Since the octahedron thus produced has a volume of four tetrahedra, and since we have learned that each tetrahedron is one energy quantum unit, Goldy has put one quantum and one quantum together to produce four quanta. Another quantum leap is demonstrated. What Goldy finds equally exciting is to realize that each of the two tetrahedra combining to make the octahedron can consist of the eight unique combinations of the black and white triangular faces and their four red, green, yellow, and blue center dots. This means an octahedron of eight black triangles, eight white, and one of four white plus four black, and the alternation of the four different color dots into all the possible combinations of eight produces four times twenty-six, which is the 104 possible combinations—where N = 8 and there are four sets of eight the formula for the number of combinations is $4 \left(\frac{N^2 - N}{2} \right)$. This result has a startling proximity to the ninety-two unique regenerative chemical elements plus their twelve additional non-self-regenerative isotopes. The bears applaud.

When the celestial approbation subsides, Goldy tries putting a light inside a translucent tetrahedron. Next she encloses the illuminated, translucent tetrahedron inside a translucent, plastic sphere. The light at the system's center casts the shadow lines of the tetrahedron's six edges outwardly and symmetrically onto the plastic sphere to produce the outlines of a spherical tetrahedron. Goldy draws circles around each of the spherical tetrahedron's four corners of such a unit radius that each of the four circles is tangent to each of the three others. Using a sharp-edged cutting tool she severingly follows around the perimeter of one circle to its point of tangency with the next adjacent circle, and there she inflects her cutting tool to follow around that next tangent circle to its next point of tangency, where she once more inflects her cutting tool's severance-trace to follow around the next circle to reach the next tangent point. She repeats this procedure until finally returning to the point of origin she completes the severance and cuts the spherical tetrahedron's surface apart in two similar equi-area sections, each of which corresponds to the two similar, dumbbell-profiled, skin sections of a baseball. With these two similar, half-a-sphere-surface sections precessingly aimed toward one another in such a manner that the bulge of one section registers symmetrically with the half-circle valley on the other, Goldy finds that she can sew the edges of the sections together around a core to produce a baseball.

Goldy shows the bears that when you look at the baseball with the inflection point of its "S" pattern "stitching" located at the circle's center and aimed directly toward you, you will see that the baseball's surface pattern is the same inflection pattern as that of the most profound Oriental symbol—yin-yang.

This observation makes Goldy say to the bears that it would seem that long ago human minds of the Orient had discovered precession, tetrahedra, and synergy. Goldy says that those ancient people who had discovered those principles must have kept them secret to surprise people and thereby gain powerful, popular, mystical accreditation and that during the ensuing millennia humanity had lost track of the yin-yang significance. Daddy Bear answers, "We have been watching the humans since they landed on your planet a few millions of years ago and can say that is just what happened."

Intrigued with her necklace experiment's discovery that squares and cubes are unstable and that only triangles are structures, and also intrigued with discovery of the way in which the geometrical behaviors of energy events can interact precessionally to quantitatively multiply themselves in pure principle, Goldy goes on to discover that multiplying numbers by themselves can be identified not only with the rate at which the number of similar squares multiply within a modularly subdivided square but also with the rate at which the number of triangles multiply within a modularly subdivided triangle, accomplished by a symmetrical and modularly uniform three-way grid, subdividing any triangularly bound area. A triangle whose edge module is two has a two-times-two-equals-four-triangles area. A triangle with edge module three contains nine similar triangles. Edge four contains sixteen similar triangles, edge five contains twenty-five similar triangles, and so on. Whereas this phenomenon of "second powering" of numbers has always heretofore been identified (even by all scientists) only with "squares," Goldy saw that a square consists of two triangles and that identifying the product of a given number multiplied by itself only with "squaring" requires twice as much area as does "triangling" and is therefore inefficient. Since she has been assured by physicists that Nature always employs the most economical (or least effort) solutions to its problems, Goldy decides to adopt "triangling" as her method of accounting area experiences and discoveries.

Goldy then discovers that a second multiplying of a number by itself (i.e., $2 \times 2 \times 2 = 8$) as a method of volumetric accounting can be identified with the rate of omni-symmetrical expansive growth of tetrahedra, whereas scholars, including scientists, have always identified this third powering of a number exclusively with the rate at which cubes multiply themselves when symmetrically amassed in an arithmetical progression of the overall cubes' symmetrically and modularly divided edges.

Goldy finds that each cube has six square faces which, being structurally unstable, collapse but which can be subdivided into two triangles each by the six diagonals that bisect each of the cube's square faces. The six diagonals are produced by omni-interconnecting four of the cube's eight corners—two of the opposite top corners with each other, and the latter with each of the two diagonally opposite bottom corners as well as interconnecting the latter two bottom corners with each other.

Not only do the six omni-interconnected diagonals of the six faces of the cube structurally stabilize the cube with minimum effort by omni-triangulation, but those diagonals are seen by Goldy also to be the six edges *AB, AC, AD, BC, BD, CD* of the tetrahedron, which Goldy has already found to be not only the minimum structural system of Universe but also to be one quantum unit of the quanta mathematics of the physicists.

Using the tetrahedron as her unit of volumetric accounting, Goldy also discovers that the volume of the equi-edged octahedron is exactly four times that of the tetrahedron. She discovered this by using the octahedron's three symmetrical *XYZ* axes running between the octahedron's six vertexes, which cross one another at ninety-degree angles at the center of volume of the octahedron. Goldy extracts the eight, one-eighth-octahedron, asymmetrical tetrahedra formed between the volumetric center point of the octahedron and each of the eight external triangular faces of the octahedron. Each of these one-eighth-octahedra has one equiangular face and three other isosceles-triangular faces, (one ninety-degree corner and two forty-five-degree corners each). Because the octahedron has a volume exactly four times that of the regular equiangular tetrahedron.

Goldy takes four of these one-eighth-octahedra, each having a volume half that of the tetrahedron ($4 \times \frac{1}{2} = 2$), and unites them symmetrically with the regular tetrahedra by matching the four one-eighth-octahedra's equiangular triangle faces with the four equiangular triangle faces of the regular tetrahedra. This produces a polyhedron of four ninety-degree corners and four other corners of $45° + 45° = 90°$ each. This is, of course, the eight-cornered cube with its structurally stabilizing, six-faces-diagonaling, six-edged tetrahedron as its core. Having added four one-eighth octahedra with a total volume of two to one tetrahedron of a volume of one, we find that the cube has a volume of exactly three times that of its structure-guaranteeing, one-quantum tetrahedron.

Goldy says that it is obviously necessary for Nature to use the tetrahedron as its volumetric accounting unit since Nature always insists on being most economical in all she does, and to use cubes for volumetric accounting obviously requires three times as much space as do tetrahedra. One important reason why less than one percent of humanity comprehends and copes effectively with science is because the three-dimensional, exclusively perpendicular and parallel, X, Y, Z, centimeter-gram second system uses three times as much space as is necessary and exhausts geometrical demonstrability with two-thirds more of Universe as yet to be identified. Science at present copes with this dilemma by use of complex, "imaginary numbers," the "square" root of minus one, etc. The fourth-dimensional behaviors of energy as black body radiation cannot be demonstrated within physics' exclusively three-dimensional model. Goldy and the bears agree that by employing Nature's own convergent-divergent, sixty-degree-angled, vectorially structured, triangular and tetrahedronal, four-dimensional coordination, all scientific knowledge can be conceptually, rationally, holistically, and therefore sensibly comprehended by all humanity. With the tetrahedron's volume as one, the cube's volume is three, the octahedron's is four, the rhombic dodecahedron's is six, and the vector equilibrium's (the old cubo-octahedron) is twenty—an omni-rational accounting system.

Goldy remembers that the philosopher Emerson said, "Poetry is saying the most important things in the simplest way." So Goldy says, "Obviously, whatever Nature does is omni-important, and since Nature is always doing whatever it does in the most economical ways, everything Nature says is poetry. If what Nature is doing is described in the most economical words, the description too is poetry." Goldy would rather have one poetically right word than a dozen familiar but inadequate words of prose. "Goldy, you are approaching our thinkable communication system when you reason that way," Wee Bear says.

Suddenly Goldy realizes that all these discoveries she has been making combine to explain how it can be that the stars of the billions of now-discovered galaxies are giving off energies at incredible rates in such a manner that as discrete quanta of energy they become discontinued and apparently annihilated, yet the same quanta of energies reappear elsewhere, as for instance in the terrestrial vegetation's photosynthetic reduction and proliferation of hydrocarbon molecules in biologic organisms and in crystallographic growths.

Since the pattern of two most dominant, critical-proximity, mass-interattraction (gravity) forces pulling diametrically on any one body produces the same model as that of Goldy's water-filled rubber tube, the precessional squeezing of a symmetrical body such as that of an octahedron by two diametric gravitational forces pulling embracingly upon it as it passes between two neighboring cosmic bodies will cause some part of the octahedron's integral, vectorial structure to yield precessionally in a plane oriented at right angles to the line between the two pulling forces, thus to transform the octahedron from its symmetrical form into an asymmetrical form. This is most economically accomplished by one of the octahedron's equatorial vector-edges disconnecting at both of its equatorially engaged end vertexes and rotating precessionally ninety degrees to rejoin its two ends with the octahedron's two polar vertexes. This local rotation results in the disappearance of the symmetrical octahedron and leaves in its stead the asymmetrical, face-bonded, three-tetrahedra assembly in the form of an arc, which is the neutral electromagnetic-wave-initiating state.

The asymmetrical arc-wave consists of the same twelve vector edges and the same eight equiangle triangles and the same six vertexes as those of the original octahedron. Topologically described, it is the same polyhedron. However, it is clearly observable that the transformation not only converted omni-directional symmetry into two-directional asymmetry, it also reduced the octahedron's exact volume of four quanta to a volume of exactly three quanta in the form of the three face-interbonded tetrahedra. What has happened here is that matter (as the symmetric, crystalline octahedron) is precessionally transformed into a directionally oriented electromagnetic wave, which upon interference with other radiation or matter will again be precessionally transformed back into the crystallographic form of the octahedron, thus syntropically regaining not only its symmetry but the one tetrahedron quantum of energy it had entropically lost.

Goldy realizes that the scientist Boltzman had long ago hypothesized that the physical universe of energy as matter was able to export energies entropically from all the stars only because those energies were being importingly reassembled syntropically in vast numbers of elsewheres. Einstein, too, assumed the foregoing to be true. However, many scientists remained skeptical, saying that entropy was universal and increasingly disorderly and expansive, whereby Universe is spending itself inexorably and irrevocably. Since photons show that energy occurs only in discrete packages and is discontinuous, and since the stars lose energy quanta entropically, how can the lost quanta reappear elsewhere? Goldy says to the bears,

"Vectorial geometry conceptually demonstrates the exact way in which energy quanta are lost and regained in the course of the entropic/syntropic turn-around events of astrophysics. The topological integrity of vectorial geometry elucidates both the one quantum loss and one quantum of energy recovery incidental to the entropic transforming from matter to radiation and the syntropic transforming from radiation to matter as clearly manifest in the octahedron to tetra-arc transformation and its reversal to the octahedron. This topological transformation (but not its energy-quantum relationship) was originally discovered in 1951 by the geodesic engineer-scientist, D. L. Richter.

"This elucidation of the way in which universe can temporarily drop out or regain its energy quanta elucidates much more," says Goldy. "It explains what happens in the photosynthetic process as planet earth's vegetation converts sun radiation receipts into beautiful hydrocarbon molecules. Energy quanta are regained on earth. It explains even more. It shows how the weightless metaphysical tetrahedron is lost and regained in universe as life dies out here and is reborn there. It shows how the triple-bonded addition of the recoverable one tetrahedron when added to the neutral phase ("W" profiled, tetra-arc, triple-bonded assembly of three tetrahedra) must always produce either a male or a female twisting helix, which when extended becomes the DNA-RNA tetrahelix, which is the structural system programmer of all living species and individuals of those species.

Impressed by Goldy's comprehension of one of their most important celestial "facts of life," the bears say to her, "Can you still further elucidate precession in a manner that always corresponds exactly with the information acquired only through humans' brain-coordinated, experience-sensing system?" Goldy replies that she thinks she can, and proceeds to so demonstrate to the bears.

Goldy first calls the bears' attention to an athlete who competes as a "hammer"-thrower. The "hammer" is a heavy steel ball attached to the "far" end of a steel rod at the "near" end of which there is a pair of triangularly shaped handles. Taking hold of the handles, each with one hand, and keeping his feet on one side of a marker bar, the "hammer" thrower accelerates the heavy "hammer" ball into a circular orbit, rotating his body by his leg muscles. He finds that the energy he puts into the orbital acceleration of the "hammer" is cumulative. The scientists speak of this as "angular momentum." Using his muscle, he can rotate faster and faster, which accelerates the ball so greatly that it no longer tends to yield immediately to gravity. The faster the thrower orbits it, the farther the "hammer" elevates, until it is circling around at his shoulder height. Then he adds in a final lift force at ninety degrees to the orbiting momentum plane just as he deliberately lets go of the handles. The more power he has skillfully invested, the farther above the horizontal will the "hammer" travel as "linear momentum" before gravity progressively overpowers it, slows it, and finally pulls it to the ground.

Leaving the "hammer" thrower, Goldy experiments with an individual who has a pea-shooter—a tube whose diameter is slightly greater than that of the uniform-diameter, plastic peas to be blown through the tube. The peashooter tube is mounted in a fixed horizontal position by attaching it to a rigidly anchored tripod stand. It is mounted in a room where there are no air currents. With his mouth full of peas the "shooter" starts blowing them in the fixed horizontal direction, which is axis Y of Goldy's experiment. This Y axis is at right angles to Goldy's line of view. The peas pass from Goldy's left to right. The projected peas exiting the tube horizontally describe a progressively descending trajectory as gravity gradually deflects each pea toward ultimate touchdown from its original horizontal of travel.

If the experimenter blows a little harder, the pea will go farther—it, too, can gain momentum from progressive initial energy investment in the act of blowing. The pea will travel ever shorter distances as the blower reduces the force of blowing. But short or long the peas all travel curvilinearly in one fixed, vertical plane, described by two separate forces acting upon them after the initial blowing: (1) the resistance of the air, (2) the earthward pull of gravity.

Aided by another bracket-mounted, screw-controlled, horizontally protrudable, steel "finger" pointing perpendicularly away from Goldy in axis X with its tip at the same height as the centerline of the peashooting tube's exit trajectory, Goldy experiments by intruding the mechanically controlled finger one-sixteenth of an inch distance into the peashooter's one-quarter-inch-in-diameter trajectory. As each pea hits the trajectory-intruding finger and is deflected angularly sidewise (away from Goldy)—each pea's trajectory in exactly the same angular amount. Gravity continues to pull the trajected peas earthward in the same manner as it did before the deflecting steel finger was intruded. Therefore, the peas continue traveling in a new but as yet vertical plane that is angled away from Goldy a slight amount around vertical axis Z, which is common to both the new vertical plane and the earlier vertical plane of the previously undeflected peas. Goldy next discovers that by progressively intruding her "finger" precessionally (forwardly away from herself) along axis X horizontally and at right angles to both the peashooter's axis Y and to the vertical axis Z, her touching of the trajectoried peas produces rotation of the also gravity-precessed vertical plane described by the peas' trajectories as rotated around vertical axis Z.

This demonstrates that once a pea has been deflected, it continues in the same horizontal compass direction and does not have a memory that tries to return it to its previous course, and that the interference deflection has no impelment momentum—it gives a discrete angular change of the trajectory, no more, no less. In the first phase of the described trajectories each pea is being separately and successively governed by four primary forces: (1) the initial, but not sustained, blown-air impelment; (2) the horizontally aimed guidance of the peashooter's tubing; (3) the continuously applied vertical deflective force of gravity; (4) the resistance of the air. In the second trajectory phase a fifth force is added: (5) the noncontinuing, single-instance, horizontal deflection of the intruding finger.

If the horizontally intruding finger were mechanically actuated to intrude slowly but continuously from the right-hand side of the trajectory, the horizontal deflection of successively deflected individual peas would find each pea descending in a new vertical plane, each a little to the left of the previous one, until the intruding finger crossed the centerline of the tube's aim, which would result in the impelled peas being stopped altogether in their horizontal paths, each bouncing backward slightly toward the tube and then yielding entirely to gravity as it falls ever faster toward the ground.

What we are learning is that each pea's course is individually altered to conform exactly to the last applied force. There is no remembered inclination to return to any previous governance by any forces operating upon the trajected unit from outside itself.

Goldy starts the air gun's impelment of the rotatable shaft's turbo-blades, and the "grass-skirt" ring of balls rises to a vigorously maintained horizontality of rotation. Goldy lowers a mechanically guided steel finger to touch downwardly, around axis Y, once only on the top of each of the balls as each passes horizontally and tangentially by the point in the plane of rotation nearest to Goldy. Each separate ball is deflected downward a discrete angular amount, which results in the plane of the balls' rotation tilting downward to the right around axis X as the powerful angular momentum of the balls' pulling outwardly on the rotating shaft causes the shaft to rotate rightwardly from its previous verticality in plane C, having rotated the same discrete angular amount as that which the plane of the rotating balls has deflected downwardly and to the right around axis X to accommodate maintenance of its tensionally enforced perpendicularity to the plane of the balls' rotation. Thus in turn, the inner rotatable annular ring in which the shaft is mounted is forced to accommodate the shaft's reorientation, and it rotates the same exact angular amount around axis X in plane C as the angular change of the plane of the rotating balls and the shaft. Goldy stops the rotation and returns the shaft and inner annular ring to their vertical starting point, with the same "grass skirt" of attached balls hanging down limply around the shaft. Once again Goldy starts the air gun's blowing of the turbo-blades. She finds that as she pulls the top of the annular ring rotationally toward herself around axis Y, it refuses to yield toward her and yields instead only leftward, as its rotating shaft and the plane of the rotating balls all tilt rightward and downward around axis X, X' as before in plane C in a direction at right angles to the plane of rotation of her pulling. With the machine in static (motionless condition) Goldy pulls the top of the vertical shaft toward her, and both it and the inner and outer rings immediately rotate toward her around axis Y between the two main stanchions.

STONE 8

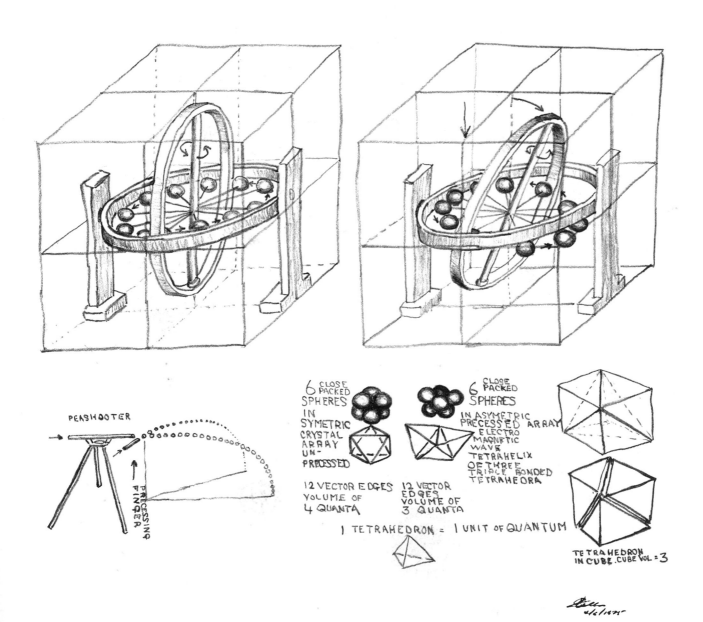

PEASHOOTER

PRECESSING FINGER

6 CLOSE PACKED SPHERES IN SYMETRIC CRYSTAL ARRAY UN-PRECESSED

6 CLOSE PACKED SPHERES IN ASYMETRIC PRECESSED ARRAY ELECTRO MAGNETIC WAVE TETRAHELIX OF THREE TRIPLE BONDED TETRAHEDRA

12 VECTOR EDGES VOLUME OF 4 QUANTA

12 VECTOR EDGES VOLUME OF 3 QUANTA

1 TETRAHEDRON = 1 UNIT OF QUANTUM

TETRAHEDRON IN CUBE . CUBE VOL = 3

Goldy notes the complete difference between a fixed-position finger's single-instance deflection and the progressively advancing, continually downward-pulling force applied to the trajectory by gravity. A crosswind would produce a continuing horizontal deflection force. If the originally fixed, horizontally impelled trajectory is continually altered by both gravity and a continuing crosswind, the succession of individually impelling forces results in a pattern of both horizontally and vertically curved trajectories altogether producing a downwardly-and-sidewise, spiraling trajectory similar to the tilted-and-bent, trailing-lower-edge feather shapes of a swiftly rotating lawn sprinkler.

Goldy now introduces another complex instructional device she calls "the precession demonstrator." First she installs two immovable, rigid, vertical steel columns four feet high and four feet apart. Between them, at a height of two feet, she mounts, in ball bearings, a horizontal steel annular ring three feet in outside diameter. The ring is dynamically balanced and free to be continuously rotated between its two supporting columns or to stop in any angular position without any predilection to further alter its angular orientation.

Inside the first ring and at two diametric points ninety degrees away from that first ring's two outer ball bearing trunnions, Goldy mounts a second and smaller ring two and a half feet in diameter. This second inner ring's two outer trunnions are also mounted in ball bearings. This inner ring is also dynamically balanced and, if desirable, free to be continually rotated inside the outer ring or to stop in any position without further momentum prejudice. Inside the inner ring and at two diametrically opposed points, each ninety degrees away from the inner ring's outside trunnion bearings, Goldy mounts a rotatable steel shaft in two end-thrust controlling, tapered roller bearings.

With everything described assembled into the machine and in proven "good working order," Goldy rotates this central roller bearing shaft and its inner annular ring into a vertical position, with the outer or base ring in a horizontal position. Goldy now shows the bears that her machine has three axes of rotation symmetrically arrayed perpendicular to one another as those three axes intersect at her machine's exact center. The X axis runs horizontally from mid-front center to mid-back of the machine. The Y axis runs horizontally from the-right-hand-side to the-left-hand-side of the machine, and the Z axis from mid-top to mid-bottom of the machine. The plane running horizontally from back to front of her machine, which plane is normal to both the X and Z axes Goldy calls plane A. The plane running vertically from front to back normal to both X and Z axes she calls the B plane and the plane running perpendicularly from right side to left side, normal to both Y and Z axes she calls plane C. "That's quite a machine, Goldy," says Mommy Bear, "Quite a lot for a little girl to produce." Goldy replies, "If you know by experience that what you are thinking works, you can reliably and realistically produce such devices in your image-ination."

In ships of the sea this complex machine, imagined by Goldy to mountingly accommodate three-independent-axial freedoms, of rotation, is called a "gimbal." Before development of modern liquid or air-support mountings ships' magnetic or gyroscopic compasses were mounted in such gimbals.

Now Goldy also mounts a set of air-turbine blades around one end of the central shaft. After that, close above the complex gimballing, she mounts the nozzle of a high-volume air gun aimed tangentially at the shaft end's turbine blades, the air jet having the ability to rotate the central shaft of goldy's machine at high velocity. The compressed air is led to the set through the interconnected hollow bearings, hollow rings, and hollow stanchions of her machine with this air ducting connected to a tank of compressed air kept at an even pressure by a compressor.

With the rotatable shaft in the vertical position, Goldy hangs twelve steel balls with equal-length woven, prestretched, flexible, stainless steel cables symmetrically positioned around the mid-shaft girth to provide a "grass skirt"-like ring of steel balls, the balls being of such a diameter that when all are radially extended, each one is tangent to each of its two horizontally adjacent neighboring balls. Goldy starts the air gun's impelment of the rotatable shaft's turbo-blades, and the "grass-shirt" ring of balls rises to a vigorously maintained horizontality of rotation.

Goldy lowers a mechanically guided steel finger that is rotating downwardly, around axis Y, to touch once only on the top of each of the balls as each passes horizontally and tangentially by the point in the plane of rotation nearest to Goldy. Each separate ball is deflected downward a discrete angular amount, which results in the plane of the balls' rotation being progressively tilted downward to the right around axis X as the powerful angular momentum of the balls' pulling outwardly on the rotating shaft causes the shaft to rotate (rightwardly at its top, leftwardly at its bottom) from its previous verticality in plane C, having rotated the same discrete angular amount as that which the plane of the rotating balls has deflected downwardly and to the right around horizontally, fore and aft axis X to accommodate maintenance

45

of its tensionally enforced perpendicularity to the plane of the balls' rotation. Thus in turn, the inner rotatable annular ring in which the shaft is mounted is forced to accommodate the shaft's reorientation, and it rotates the same exact angular amount around axis X in plane C as the angular change of the plane of the rotating balls and the shaft. Intent to better understand the transformation logic of this precessional behavior, Goldy stops the rotation and returns the shaft and inner annular ring to their vertical starting point, with the same "grass skirt" of attached balls hanging down limply around the shaft. Once again Goldy starts the air gun's blowing of the turbo-blades.

This time, instead of touching downwardly (in plane B) upon the swiftly and horizontally rotating balls nearest to her, Goldy takes hold of the top of the inner annular ring just above the rotating shaft's top bearing and pulls that point toward herself in plane B, pulling around horizontally, left to right, axis Y as she stands in front of the machine. To her now-dawning comprehension of what is transpiring precessionally, she finds that as she pulls the top of the annular ring rotationally toward herself around axis Y, it refuses to yield toward her and yields instead only leftward, which is clockwise to Goldy, as its rotating shaft and the plane of the rotating balls all tilt rightward and downward around axis X, X' as before in plane C in a direction at right angles to the plane of rotation of her pulling. This time Goldy finds that as long as she continues pulling, the whole system keeps rotating clockwise in plane C. If she stops pulling, it ceases rotation. If she resumes pulling the top of the machine's annular ring toward herself, it again refuses to yield toward her, and instead the rotating shaft plus the plane of the balls' rotation plus the inner annular ring all tilt rightward and downward clockwise around axis X, X' in a plane C in a direction at right angles to fore and aft, vertical plane B or her would-be but frustrated pulling around horizontally left to right axis Y. The harder she pulls, the faster do the always congruently moving three-member group of (1) balls, (2) shaft, and (3) inner annular ring continue to rotate clockwise around the horizontal, fore and aft X axis in the vertical, left-to-right plane of rotation C—and they keep on doing so as long as Goldy keeps on pulling toward herself on the inner annular ring adjacent to the rotatable shaft end bearing. This is because her applied force is now a continuing and increasing force and not a single touch-impulse as before. At first this behavior seemed superficially perverse—with the system yielding only at right angles to the force of Goldy's pulling toward herself.

To prove to herself and the bears the difference between the dynamic and static behavior of her "precession machine," Goldy stops the air power and allows the cable-connected balls and their shaft to stop rotating. She then returns the central shaft and its annular ring to the vertical position and the outer ring to the horizontal. Now, with the machine in static (motionless condition) Goldy pulls the top of the vertical shaft toward her, and both it and the inner and outer rings immediately rotate toward her around axis Y between the two main stanchions of the machine as the cable-connected balls dangle center-of-earthward. Now she pushes the whole rig back into the same vertical starting position as for all the previous tests. Taking off the "grass skirt" of steel balls, she substitutes a solid flywheel around the mid-girth of the central shaft. Next, without air-starting the machine, she touches downwardly on the point of the flywheel nearest to her in front of the machine in exactly the same way she had touched down on each of the (air-and-shaft) accelerated steel balls. This time the shaft and wheel are not rotating, and therefore have no angular momentum. The "solid" flywheel, the shaft, and both the annular rings tip forwardly toward Goldy around axis Y of the system. She now once again opens the air power and accelerates the shaft and "solid" flywheel into swift rotation. Once again she touches on top of the wheel at the same, nearest-to-her, front-of-the-machine point at which she had touched each swiftly rotating steel ball of the "grass skirt" experiment, and this time the wheel and inner annular ring (but not the outside ring) rotate clockwise rightwardly and downwardly around axis X, just as did the succession of shaft-tethered balls in all the other dynamic experiments. Thus Goldy feels the difference between the static, no-momentum behavior of the unaccelerated system and that of the dynamic behavior of the accelerated, angular-momentum-dominated system. The flywheel's atoms (but not the annular rings, shaft, and stanchions) attain such an acceleration as to render negligible the pull of gravity upon the outer rotating mass of the wheel. Gravity, however, pulls unopposedly earthward upon the nonrotating members of the machine.

As Professor Goddard realized, the earth rotating at an equatorial speed of 1,000 nautical miles per hour is itself also moving around the sun at 60,000 miles an hour. Goddard also realized that a pre-blast-off rocket uprightly poised on earth also travels congruently with the earth at 60,000 mph around the sun and, like a chip on a walking man's shoulder, remains only seemingly "at rest" in respect to its larger companion-in-motion. If we "blast off" the rocket, accelerating it to a speed much greater than that of both the earth's axial rotation and its sun-orbiting speed, then according to Newton's and Galileo's laws, every time the rocket doubles its distance away from the earth, the tendency to fall back to earth is reduced to one quarter of the previous tendency, and soon, if the original acceleration was adequate, or if it is boosted by a second stage firing, the rocket will get so far out from earth as no longer to tend to fall back earthward and will yield to the equilibriously integrated earth's, sun's, moon's, and all other stars' pulls, and thereafter, if beyond the earth's outermost mantle's frictional interferences and resultant retardations, will maintain its own independent orbit around the earth.

Earth's gravity is rendered progressively less effective as acceleration is increased. That acceleration can be rotational as well as "linear." That is, it can be angularly accelerated, as with the cable-connected balls of Goldy's machine, or linearly, as with the hammer thrower's cumulatively accelerated and released hammer. When the hammer thrower's steel ball (hammer) is released from its six-foot radius of human rotation, it comes to rest on the earth, where it orbits in a vastly greater circle around the earth's axis as the latter orbits in a ninety-two-million-mile radiused circle around the sun, whereby we learn that the so-called linear acceleration, as contrasted to so-called rotational (or angular) acceleration, is always rotational but of vastly different radius. The relative reduction-of-gravity effect attained by acceleration, Goldy explains, is the same whether rotationally or linearly accomplished. That is why a swiftly rotating gyroscope in a three-ring cage with a sharp bottom-of-system support point can be concentratedly base-supported on a pencil's rubber end while leaning sidewise, not falling farther sidewise and floorward as would the same assembly when static (i.e., with its flywheel not rotating). Goldy explains that it is the linear acceleration of a bicycle that converts it from the static condition of lying prone on the ground when motionless to maintaining as vertical an attitude as possible, and the faster it goes, the more "muscularly" vertical does it become and the more does it tend to leave the earth altogether, as is manifest in the motorcyclist swiftly returning to the vertical after leaning sidewise to produce a steering effect. This outward-from-earth-center's force keeps the bicycle's center of gravity as far out from the earth's center as is possible, while the residual but diminishing gravitational effect is residually apparent only as the integrated weight of the whole bicycle and rider are concentrated at the two points where the bicycle wheels' tires touch the road. For this reason swiftly moving cyclists muscularly accumulating their momentum can ride around in a bowl, climbing its sides until reaching a horizontal attitude as they circle inside the top cylinder of the bowl. This dynamic horizontal stability is the same as that of the spinning gyroscope leaning horizontally outward from the pencil end with all the earthward gravity pull being exerted only at the support point as it rests on the pencil's rubber end.

What occurs in the dynamic rotational phase of Goldy's "precession machine" can be readily understood when we go back to both the peashooter and to the hammer thrower who lets go of his hammer handles not when they, and the hammer, are pointing in the direction he wishes the hammer to travel but at the point when the hammer and its handles are pointing sidewise at right angles to the direction in which the thrower wants the hammer to go. (Because people

48

know only that a centrifuge separates cream from milk, they think of centrifugal separation as occurring outwardly in a radial line perpendicular to the rotating perimeter of the centrifuge, whereas the separation is always tangential to the spinning perimeter, which means at a right angle to the centrifuge's radius end.)

Both the peas of the peashooting experiment and the steel balls of Goldy's machine experiment acted in exactly the same way, simply altering their planes of trajectory with those planes being reoriented around the same axis X an angular amount exactly proportional to that given by the single momentary deflection impulse given perpendicular to the original trajectory with that impulse administered downwardly around axis Y. "No mystery," says Goldy. "Everything behaves as carefully reconsidered experience says it does. Nothing is perverse except humans' natural propensity for trying to explain dynamic interrelationships while thinking only of static models."

The machine that Goldy had built is called a gyroscope: *gyro-scopus* meaning "making visual the complex behaviors of dynamically rotating complexes."

Goldy says to the bears that her previously shared popular mis-sensing of the gyroscope's behavior as being perverse did not take into account the cumulative dynamism of angular momentum and anticipated only a static system's unacceleratedly yielding behavior. Thus Goldy comprehended that many of the experiences humanity has heretofore failed to understand can now be realistically understood as aided by such experimentally followed-through sensing of each of the combined behaviors of complexedly operative dynamic systems, and furthermore, all systems are dynamical and can only be comprehended as such—with the comprehender always aware that everything seemingly "at rest" is in congruent motion with its greater-momentum host. The bears concur, saying also that Universe is an omnidynamic operation that only deceptively seems to be motionless as little humans, like microbes on a large flywheel, fail to feel the wheel's rotation. Humans on planet earth at the latitude of New York City are revolving around earth's axis at about 700 miles per hour as their planet earth zooms orbitally around the sun at 60,000 miles per hour, doing it so efficiently and smoothly that it makes no sounds, which allows humans' static ego to misperceive the sun to be 'setting' and earth to be 'standing still.' "

"From where we view you it seems incredible to us that you can't feel your own motion," say the astonished bears. "Your earth planet's unretarded momentuming at 60,000 miles per hour in frictionless space within critical proximity of the sun-star's massive gravitational pull, tethers onrushing earth like a lassoed steer so that it can only go thereafter in a gravity-retained orbit around the sun."

Coming in at this juncture, Daddy bear says that what Goldy has experienced would hold true in the case of a regular gyroscope and its regular (fallaciously described as "solid") flywheel, which is an aggregate of all the energy quanta of all the atoms, which act together just as did the individual steel balls when accelerated in her machine.

Goldy realizes that humans spontaneously misinform themselves in many directional matters because by twisting their necks they can look in preferred directions without also rotating their bodies. While wishing to propel an object in the "looked-at" direction, humans say that they are throwing or hitting the object to be propelled in that direction, whereas in operational fact, to send a tennis ball to the opposite court the player throws the ball vertically upward above his head—that is, in a direction at a right angle to the direction he wishes to send the ball—and then hits the ball only when the tennis racquet and his human arm propelling it are also pointed in a direction overhead, which is exactly at a right angle to the direction that the ball is to go. The baseball player lets go of the ball only when it is at the farthermost point of arm-swing away at a right angle from the direction he wishes the ball to go. The fact that the individual can consciously turn his head and eyes in directions at right angles to the subconsciously organized orientation of his body to produce the most cumulative energy effectiveness as well as the most accurate angular spin control, both of which occur subconsciously in a direction at right angles to that which he thinks he is facing, often fools individuals into thinking that they are really throwing balls in the direction they are facing—subconsciously remembering that when they wanted to push something in front of them away from themselves, they shoved it away perpendicularly with their arms or with a hand-held poking stick. Atrociously performing, untutored tennis novices often start their ineffective playing by facing only forward and trying to push-hit the ball forwardly in front of them, producing only a bounce-back or poke-back return of the ball. However, if the novices are fortunate enough to begin with a good professional tennis teacher, they will learn to jump into backhand or forehand positions, facing sharply at right angles away from the direction they wish to send the ball. Both the baseball batter and the golfer stand sidewise to the desired trajectory and hit the ball when it is exactly at a right angle away from the player's desired direction of ball impelment. The reason both the golfer and baseball batter "follow through" with their bat or club swing after hitting the ball is to avoid putting any sidewise pushing or pulling spin on the ball at the moment of sidewise impact, which spin could misdirect or shorten the distance of accomplished trajectory. The athletes are taught to "follow through" because the action and sequence of events is too fast for human sensing, and the eyes and muscle have to be trained not to look in the direction they want the ball to go, but at the point where the critical action takes place at right angles to that line of impelment—where the angular momentum is transferred from the rotating arm, club, bat, or racquet to the free-to-travel ball.

Goldy remarks to the bears that since everything in Universe is in motion, the interactivation of all the macro and micro islands of energy of Universe are precessional, and because precession is not popularly understood, humanity is at yet generally in ignorance regarding almost everything that goes on; but because of the vanity employed by ignorance to cover lack of knowledge, humanity talks about problem-solving as though humans were the only ones in Universe capable of coping with important problems. The bears say to Goldy, "Even the earthian scientists have coped with precession only by use of theoretical mathematics, quantum mechanics, and without any personal sensing of the logical integrity of the phenomenon." Earthian science has mistakenly thought it to be impossible to elucidate precession conceptually and exclusively in the terms of directly sensed human experience.

Because all bodies of Universe are either closely or remotely restrained by a plurality of mass inter-attractiveness always and continuously coexisting between themselves and other bodies in Universe, there can be no truly straight linear acceleration. There will always be only angular acceleration of vastly varying radii of restraint, often producing arcs of circles so great as to seem locally straight. But linear momentum is only "theoretically potential" it is made "eternally impossible" by the always-and-forever, unity-is-plural "otherness" inherent in Universe. "That was what probably occasioned Einstein's 'curved space,' " says Goldy. The bears say, "Sounds logical, Goldy." While light and all other radiation have the same fixed speed and operate in finitely closed and quantized packages, gravity is omni-continuous and omni-embracing, but is stretched in a multiplicity of ways varying from intensely strong to ephemerally weak, but no matter how relatively weak, it maintains its never completely exhausted omni-presence and its always and everywhere embracement in degree adequate to guarantee the eternally regenerative integrity of Universe. Gravity is the omni-embracing, omni-pervasive perfection of comprehension. Gravity is cosmic love.

Goldy next shows the bears how the three-face-bonded tetrahedra-arc in its initial, neutral, nontransmitting state becomes spirally extended positively or negatively to attain its information-transmitting state, only with the addition of one more face-bonded tetrahedron. She then shows that with every twenty tetrahedra the tetrahelix completes approximately one 360 degree helical revolution (352° 40′ exactly), which tetrahelix is the mathematical model employed by the DNA-RNA helix, discovered by virological scientists (Watson-Crick-Wilkerson) to be always transmitting the specific information controlling the design of all biological species, with that 7° 20′ of angle (less than 360°) being twist-sprung to introduce the unzipping force necessary to offspring (or give birth to) any given species' off-molded offspring from the parent.

Goldy shows how the extended tetrahelix's skin can be stripped off and laid out flat as a three-row, omni-triangulated, wavilinear ribbon. Goldy then identifies the positively or negatively asymmetrical tetrahelix patterning with lightning. Goldy then introduces Naga—the sea serpent—god of the oceanic world of the ancients. Naga is the wave. Naga is a live tetrahelix. At sea the wavilinear profile of Naga's back always rims the horizon. The ancient Hebraic language of the earliest biblical scripture came to contain the word *nachash,* which means serpent, or "whisper," or "divine" (the *ch* being a guttural or g sound)—i.e., Naga and Nachashol (or Nagashol) means "the sea," and the root verb *nacha* (= *Naga*) means to "lead," "conduct," "guide," and Nacha—pronounced Naga—is also the name of the ancient seafarer N(O)(A)(C)H—Noah.

STONE 9

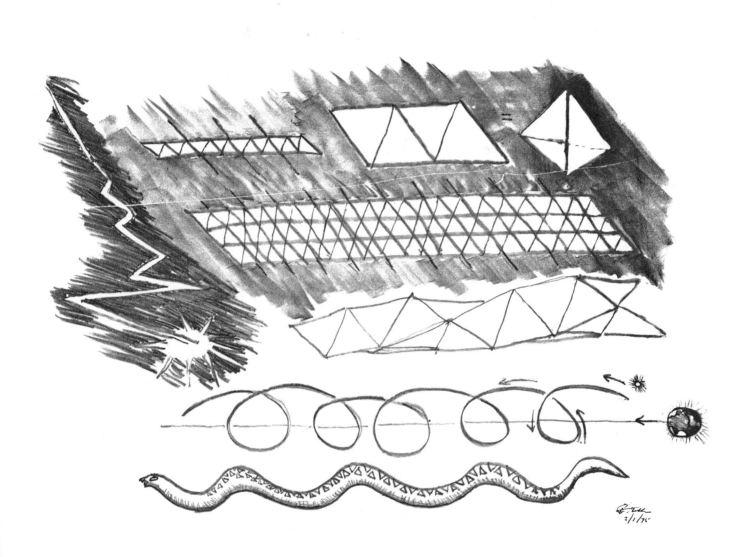

Goldy next shows the bears how the three-face-bonded tetrahedra-arc in its initial, neutral, nontransmitting state becomes spirally extended positively or negatively to attain its information-transmitting state, only with the addition of more face-bonded tetrahedra. She then shows that with every twenty tetrahedra the tetrahelix completes approximately one 360-degree helical revolution (352° 40′ exactly), which tetrahelix is the mathematical model employed by the DNA-RNA helix, discovered by virological scientists (Watson-Crick-Wilkerson) to be always transmitting the specific information controlling the design of all biological species, with that 7° 20′ of angle (less than 360°) being twist-sprung to introduce the unzipping force necessary to offspring (or give birth to) any given species' off-molded offspring from the parent.

Goldy shows how the extended tetrahelix's skin can be stripped off and laid out flat as a three-row, omni-triangulated, wavilinear ribbon. Goldy then identifies the positively or negatively asymmetrical tetrahelix patterning with lightning when, with the closure of an electron circuit from earth to cloud, the high-voltage atmospheric charges are transmitted to earth.

Goldy then introduces Naga—the sea serpent—god of the oceanic world of the ancients. Naga is the wave. Naga is a live tetrahelix. At sea the wavilinear profile of Naga's back always rims the horizon.

Influenced by the language of previous millennia of long-distance ocean-traveling sailors coming originally from the atolls of the South Pacific and Indian Ocean into the Arabian Sea to reach Mesopotamia, and by the subsequent retracing of those world-encircling deep-sea routes by the Phoenicians, the ancient Hebraic language of the earliest biblical scripture came to contain the word *nachash,* which means "serpent," or "whisper," or "divine" (the *ch* being a guttural or g sound)—i.e., Naga and Nachashol (or Nagashol) means "the sea," and the root verb *nacha* (= Naga) means "to lead," "conduct," "guide," and Nacha [pronounced "Naga"] is also the name of the ancient seafarer n (o) (a) (c)h—Noah.

Nachan (pronounced "Nagan") is the word for copper or bronze alloy, the latter being the high-strength form of the nonrustable metal with which all ship fastenings, fittings, and instruments have of necessity been fashioned since copper's first discovery and its alloyed production as bronze by humans 5,000 years ago at Ban Chiang in Thailand, where the Bronze Age first took over from the Stone Age, in what was once a Venice-like complex of canals leading from the sea into all of the Southeast Asian lowlands on the Indochina coast, nearest to all the seafaring activities of the Southwest Pacific in the region where the Naga nation long ago came off the sea and put out upon the mainland and as yet lives. Where Hanoi now exists there existed 2,000 years ago a place called Nganna.

This Bronze Age birth occurs at the final peak of the Austronesian civilization. These ancient water people's world embraced the Central and South Pacific, South Indian Ocean all the way westward to include Madagascar, and all the way eastward to include Easter Island and all the way northward to include both Japan and the Hawaiian Islands and southward to include New Zealand. This is the world of Naga, the na prefix being the na of na-vy; na-tivity; na-vi-ga-tion; na-tion; 180,000,000 of these Austronesians as yet are alive, and many are as yet living with the same maritime and insular artifacts as those of their possibly millions-of-years-ago forebears.

TRICAP 10

When the god of the sea Naga tidally enters the river mouths of the land, as seen
from the high mountain, his snake shape is clearly revealed by the river's shape. The Japanese
word for river, *Nagala,* indicates that the ancient water people looked upon the
riverbanks and beds as constituting the female organ of the land being sexually intruded by
Naga, god of the sea, as the oceanic tides pulsed inwardly and outwardly for great
distances at the lower extremities of the rivers. The early humans sensed and revered the
greater pattern events of Universe as manifesting an ever and everywhere presence of a
knowing and life-giving, supporting, and terminating competence vastly greater than that of
humans. They saw themselves and all that they could see including the sun, moon, and
stars as having only minuscule local parts in an organic whole whose shape and size
transcended both the ranges of their vision and the scope of their imagining.

STONE 10

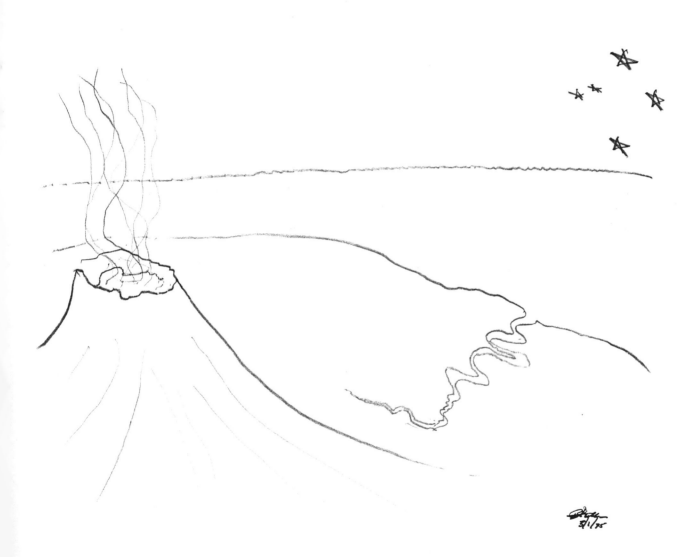

When the god of the sea Naga tidally enters the river mouths of the land, as seen from the high mountain, his snake shape is clearly revealed by the river's shape. The Japanese word for river, *nagala,* indicates that the ancient water people looked upon the riverbanks and beds as constituting the female organ of the land being sexually intruded by Naga, god of the sea, as the oceanic tides pulsed inwardly and outwardly for great distances at the lower extremities of the rivers. The early humans sensed and revered the greater pattern events of Universe as manifesting an ever and everywhere presence of a knowing and life-giving, -supporting, and -terminating competence vastly greater than that of humans. They saw themselves and all that they could see, including the sun, moon, and stars, as being only minuscule local parts in an organic whole whose shape and size transcended both the ranges of their vision and the scope of their imagining.

TRICAP 11

Goldy reasons that because all human beings are always born naked, ignorant and helpless yet chromosomally programmed to experience periodic hunger, thirst, curiosity, and the procreative urge—and are thereby provoked to search and learn only by trial and error, to discover for themselves how best to cope in general—their nakedness and organic structuring primarily 60-percent water, which requires frequent replenishment, combines with the fact of water's small temperature range between freezing and boiling to make it immediately clear that naked humans could not be born nakedly and survive north of the freezing line or in arid desert or where any large carnivorous animals could swallow their for-months-helpless babies. By far the most favorable localities and conditions for successful inauguration of human life, to be found anywhere around planet earth, would be those environmental conditions unique to the barrier-reef-encircled and mountain-island-centered coral atolls formed atop extinct volcanoes in the southern seas of the Pacific and Indian oceans. Here we have the beautiful, clear, shoal water lying protected within the circular Great Barrier reef of coral against which great ocean waves thunder and spend their massive power. Lagoons, temperatured ideally for prolonged human immersion, lie inside the reef and abound with fish and all other most ideal primitive environmental conditions for nurturing naked humans. Beautiful shoal beaches make easy walking into and out of the water while high palm-tree coconuts, full of milk, fall thumping to the ground, and humans may find a host of fruits and no wild animals. Here humans quickly learned that wood floats and stones sink.

STONE 11

With the bears' long experience to help her, Goldy speculates on how humans came to dwell on planet earth. Goldy reasons that because all human beings are always born naked, ignorant, and helpless, yet chromosomally programmed to experience periodic hunger, thirst, curiosity, and the procreative urge—and are thereby provoked to search and learn only by trial and error, to discover for themselves how best to cope in general—their nakedness and organic structuring of primarily 60 percent water, which requires frequent replenishment combines with the fact of water's small temperature range between freezing and boiling to make it immediately clear that naked humans could not be born nakedly and survive north of the freezing line or in arid desert or where any large carnivorous animals could swallow their for-months-helpless babies. By far the most favorable localities and conditions for successful inauguration of human life to be found anywhere around planet earth would be those environmental conditions unique to the barrier-reef-encircled and mountain-island-centered coral atolls formed atop extinct volcanoes in the southern seas of the Pacific and Indian oceans. Here we have the beautiful, clear, shoal water lying protected within the circular Great Barrier Reef of coral against which great ocean waves thunder and spend their massive power. Lagoons, temperatured ideally for prolonged human immersion, lie inside the reef and abound with fish and all other most ideal primitive environmental conditions for nurturing naked humans. Beautiful shoal beaches make easy walking into and out of the water, while high palm-tree coconuts, full of milk, fall thumping to the ground, and humans may find a host of fruits and no wild animals. Here humans quickly learned that wood floats and stones sink. They learned that a single floating log rolls and that two floating logs held cross-connected by their branches do not roll, but provide a structurally stable floating device from which they could fish or dive for edible mollusks. The atoll dwellers soon learned to build both multilogged rafts and dugout log boats as well as outrigger-stabilized dugout canoes. Then they learned how to stitch together the palm tree's fronds to make combined masts and sails and found that their outrigger canoes could sail zigzaggingly to windward while rafts could only ride with the ocean currents or drift to leeward with the wind. The outrigger canoes could be worked (or could "beat") to windward by a succession of individual "tackings," first leftward, then rightward, at a firmly sail-filling angle, which is about thirty degrees one side or the other of the direction from which the wind is coming. This produced a low atmospheric pressure on the forward and leeward side of their sails, which, as with twentieth-century airplane wingfoils, pulled their boats forward in the direction of least resistance, which direction could be modifyingly controlled by steering oars or paddles.

The Austronesians learned, only after millennia of experience slowly reported by those who ultimately returned home from the sea, that there are many variables and periodic reversals in the Pacific Ocean currents but that the rafts drift mostly northward, eastward, and later southward, following what is now known as the Japanese Current. This took them via the Aleutians to North American Alaska and subsequently coasting southward to Central and South America, thereafter to return them westward across the Pacific to their original atolls region with, however, another two-way trans-Pacific wind and current pattern found also to be operating in the southern regions of the Pacific. However, the atoll people learned in far shorter time that sailing canoes can beat westward into the prevailing westerly winds, thus finally to reach the Oriental mainland coast, as well as southward to the mainlands of Australia, westward to India and thence to the east coast of Africa across the Indian Ocean or northwestward in that ocean to Arabia. All these ocean routes between the atolls and the mainland coasts are shown in this picture by Goldy.

In its sky she includes the "Southern Cross" because it and the Pole Star on Mommy Bear's nose were recognized very early by the South Seas na-vi-ga-tors as providing a fixed north/south celestial axis around which spun either the spherical vessel earth or all the rest of the celestial universe. In view of their experience the former seemed more logical. Throughout history all water people experienced the omni-motion and travel of their own vessel over the curvature of the circular horizon, gradually lowering behind which in all directions they saw finally vanish islands, mountains, and other vessels, as well as the sun and the moon, as their vessels or rafts moved on. Familiar with human skulls and a myriad of spheroidal objects from pebbles to blowfish, their experience must have led them to realize that this disappearance below the horizon in all directions as observed from any point on the ocean could be interpreted only as the experience of being on a very large spheroidal celestial object. Anyone who thinks it extravagant to accredit these ancient water people with such perceptive interpretation capabilities may learn of the crucial part played by their perceptive, intuitive interpretation of the separate delicate reflex wavelets occurring amongst the tumult of larger wave complexes which tell them of the presence at various distances and in various directions of islands as yet far beyond sight. The ancient seafarers probably saw the stars vanish to the westward, i.e., lost to sight, or they saw those same stars disclosed again as the part of the sphere where the navigators were was rotated out of the line of sight to the westward of the navigators, but reversed again to the eastward by their astroship's rotation. Motion of self and one's ship always seemed normal to the water people. It may well be that the concept of the earth revolving in the sky ocean seemed as spontaneously logical to these sailors as did the rotating appearance and plunge-from-sight of whales and porpoises. To the Polynesian Maori, the sea is normal and islands are exceptional. Islands are holes-in-the-ocean. Bays are female receptacles occupied by the male sea. The sea peoples probably conceived of themselves as being aboard a great, watery-backed whale or a revolving, spherical vessel sailing through the sky. This concept is opposite to that evolved by the millions-of-years-later-to-develop, exclusively mainland-dwelling, static settlers.

To the surprise of the Three Bears, who had been watching what went on around the surface of planet earth for some billions of years, Goldy went on surmising with such comprehensively thinking logic about humanity's development on her planet that the bears found her speculative accounting of history so close to "right on" that they rarely felt any necessity to correct her. Despite that, her account differed fundamentally from the prime evolutionary concepts fostered by humanity's scholars at the beginning of the last quarter of what earthians speak of as the twentieth century. For instance, Goldy explained that the design sequence and assemblage of humanity's complexedly associated atomic elements, assembled into molecules, compounded into cells, all complexedly assembled and behaviorally programmed by chromosomal proclivities as a functioning organism, as well as the designs for progressively assembling all the other radiobeam biological members of the earthian ecology team, were programmed and transmitted from elsewhere in Universe for most favorable operation under specific environmental conditions at exact locations on planet earth. These specific species and individual design control program beamings scheduled the relative quantities of the requisite elemental atoms and the sequence of their subassociations and general organic assemblies. These cosmically originated, electromagnetic, photosynthetic programmings are exactly the same morphological control codings as those of the complexedly and uniquely intervariable sequences of the guanine-cytosine, thymine-adenine of the DNA-RNA tetrahelix assemblage programming codes and of their subsequent operational proclivities, which structural and

64

behavioral programmings (as Goldy explained earlier) were recently discovered to be governing the unique design not only of all the biological species but of all individuals within the species. All the requisite chemical constituents for exactly complying with the coded design instructions are or were present on planet earth at the time of the original electromagnetic wave reception at the terrestrial locii of species' inceptions, which are predetermined by the unique electromagnetic environment's complex tunability existing only at those locii. Many of the requisite chemical elements for tunably satisfying those cosmically originated species programs had arrived on earth at earlier times, coming as stardust or comet plume fallouts. Goldy explained that the chemical atoms are all physical whereas the phenomenon life is utterly metaphysical. Life is the fourth, now-you-see-it-and-now-you-don't quantum. The metaphysical mind employs these organically regenerative, subjectively interacting, sensing, storing, and intuiting devices as well as all the organism's unique, objectively articulate facilities to harvest critically relevant information.

Goldy points out to the bears that what has not been understood thus far by human scientists regarding the transmittal of energy from the sun to support biological life on planet earth is accomplished through the photosynthesis of sun radiation to produce hydrocarbon molecules by terrestrial vegetation and algae is that in addition to its heat-transmitting properties the radiation is also a yes-no-frequency programmed information carrier—which precessionally transforms the three-tetrahedral quanta of radiation into the four-quanta octahedral crystals in the atomic formation of the hydrocarbon molecules. Photosynthesis is meaningful communication whereby metaphysics rules the physical (like the Federal Reserve Bank) by issuing or withdrawing complex coding-identified "quanta" currency from the overall, cosmic, transforming and transaction system's accounting.

Goldy points out that the initially regenerative organismic equipment of any biological species, including humans, can be inbred to concentrate the programmed probability of dominance of certain behavioral characteristics in the offspring and that the human design as received on planet earth starts with optimum inclusion of general adaptability—ergo, humans cannot be fundamentally improved upon physically. Humans are not only halfway between the largest and smallest known biological species, but are distinguished from all other species in that all other species have predominant "built-in" equipment, giving them special physical performance advantages in special environments but prohibiting or limiting their existence in many environments. Humans can only be protected, supported, and accommodated more effectively by human mind's capability to employ abstract principles wherewith to invent and produce various artifacts that will permit humans to cope with evolutionary changes of the environment within which the humans are to function. Goldy shows that the modification of the biological organisms by inbreeding through concentration of special-type genes—for instance, the mating of two fast-running horses—increases the mathematical probability of offspring with such specialized fast-running physical behavior excellence. This progressive reduction of general adaptability always leads toward eventual extinction of that species when those bred-out, infrequent, extreme environmental conditions—adaptability to which had been sacrificed with the inbreeding—do occur.

Goldy also points out that inbreeding experience shows that human organisms could be progressively inbred to attain high probability of retaining only tree-branch-swinging simian characteristics and capabilities in the offspring while concurrently outbreeding many of the comprehensive range of human faculties and capabilities. This would require the provision of a complex of separated-out, ecological-environment-support devices or biological species whose operative presence permitted the unique specialization within the generalized cosmic complex of chemistries and frequencies of eternally regenerative Universe.

Goldy then points out that on the other hand there is no breeding experience of earthians which suggests that the limited inventory of different chemical elements constituting amoebas could be progressively amplified and complexed to produce the wide variety of chemical elements constituting the unique information-harvesting organisms employed by metaphysical humanity.

On the other hand, humans have been able to separate out and transplant hearts, kidneys, blood, skin, bones of humans, sometimes substituting mechanical devices for keeping the separated-out human constituents separately alive by remote complementary interfunctioning devices. Originally integrally complex human functions could be multiplyingly deployed into a plurality of intercomplementary functioning devices, organisms, and creatures. It is implicit that amoebas and other simple organisms can be progressively, subdivisionally isolated out of complex organisms such as those of humans and introduced into an intercomplemenentary ecological-environment-sustaining complex, but not vice versa. Goldy says

Darwin's evolutionary sequence was brilliantly conceived but its occurrence programming was in reverse of reality.

Humans are as complex as Universe. Each human is one way in which all the potential intertransformabilities, degrees of freedom, and frequency variables could eventuate, while all the other complementary evolution events of Universe concurrently transpired.

"As partially noted previously," Goldy says, "the complex physical organisms employed by exclusively metaphysical humans differ from all other species in that all other species have highly specialized, built-in, special-functioning equipment integral with their unit organisms which provide special capabilities in special environments, whereas the human organism lacks any such special integral equipment for functioning in special environments. Many creatures have brains. Brains always and only coordinatingly apprehend, store, and recall only the special-case input information provided by humans' senses: smelling, tasting, touching, hearing, seeing, and possibly an ultrahigh-frequency electromagnetic wave tune-in-ability. Brains of all the brain-equipped creatures always and only apprehend, memory-bank, and reconsider the special-case information sense-harvested from their succession of special-case experiences. In addition to their brains' special information apprehending, storing, and retrieving capability, the metaphysically operative humans have minds which have the (only intuitively triggered) exclusively unique capability of discovering the synergetic, weightless, covariant, complex interrelationships always existing only between but never in any of the separately considered special-case phenomena with which the brain is exclusively preoccupied. Human mind not only can discover the weightless, abstract, only mathematically statable, generalized scientific principles governing physical behaviors of Universe, but human mind can also use the generalized principles to produce the special-case technology with which to cope successfully within any special-case environment and do so more effectively than can those creatures with special-environment-adapted, integral equipment. Bernoulli's discovery of the principal governing behaviors of atmospheric pressure differentials led to comprehension of the negative-pressure lift produced by motion through the air on top of a wingfoil, which eventually made possible human wingfoil flight forty times faster than that of birds. When, however, humans are not using their mind- and intuition-discovered equipment, they can detach themselves from that equipment and, unburdened, can make that equipment available to others. Generalization-informed human minds can deal with any special environment, but in order to do so they have developed a myriad of detached-from-self tools and devices with which to operate more successfully not only in all the known special environments around our planet earth's surface than can any of the many known creatures especially and integrally equipped for operation in those special environments, but also occurring outside the earth's biosphere in "general space" and on the airless, waterless moon, where no other only integrally equipped species can survive. All of humanity's nonintegral, special-environment operations equipment may be employed interchangeably by all humans. Goldy remarks that apparently humans' minds have the potential capability of technically advantaging humans in sufficient degree to permit their eventual, safe, and progressively informing exploration of any and all physical and metaphysical environments in local Universe. Since "life" and its comprehending mind are only metaphysical, weightless, sizeless, and immortal, there are no physical environment conditions within which humans cannot cognitively prosper.

For these and other reasons Goldy assumes that the only-from-mind-to-mind-communicable, abstract, weightless, synergetic, pattern integrities, with which the minds of exclusively meta-physical human life operate, are utterly transcendental to any physical evolution transform-ability. In confirmation of this, Goldy notes that when human organisms are declared dead, all the physical chemistry misidentified by scientists as constituting the prime ingredients of human life are as yet present—ergo, those who speak of "the chemistry of life" are, unwittingly, self-misinforming. Life is not chemistry. Life is not physical. Life is indestructible, immortal, eternal. Life is only weightlessly and omni-invisibly present.

Goldy points out that the earliest humans who were incubated within the environment of those barrier reef-surrounded, centrally mountained, extinct volcano atolls were exposed to the sun for millions of years, during which time vitamin D combined to introduce permanent pigmentation of their sun-darkened skins—ergo, except for the soles of their feet and the palms of their hands, which were seldom exposed to the sun, the skin of the original human occupants of planet earth was dark skin.

Goldy goes on to explain that only after millennia did some humans first reach the mainland shores, where they lived for additional millennia on their rafts and boats, moored in protected waters just off the shore, so that large wild animals of the mainland could not reach them. Here during the daylight hours the humans went ashore, gradually caught and domesticated goats, sheep, horses, elephants, et al. In later millennia they pastured their flocks and learned how to live safely on the mainland, whereafter they followed as their flocks and herds grazed even farther inland and higher on the mountain slopes and wandered into increasingly cold areas. In doing so the humans learned to wear the skins of those animals whose flesh they were eating. After a million years of westward and northward peregrinations, settlings, and resettlings, some of their progeny reached the North Atlantic and Arctic Ocean shores of the Eurasian continent, thereafter settling in the cold-wintered Northern Europe. After those millions of years of cross-continent wintering and Ice Age hybernating in caves and millions of inbreedings of chieftains with their kin, plus progressive covering of their skins, the vitamin variables of their changing diets progressively allowed the more northerly and cave-beshadowed skins to bleach out—ergo the light- and white-skinned descendants of the dark-skinned ancestors gradually came into existence. Goldy points out that these human-skin pigmentation effects of cave dwelling in the various geographical latitudes and altitudes is also manifest in direct correspondence with the human skin coloring in those same latitudes and altitudes of the hardwood trees, which vary progressively from the white oaks, birch, and maples of the north through the mild darkenings of ash and walnut, then get even grayer in the teak, then even darker in the high tropics mahogany, and finally attain utter blackness in the equatorial ebonies.

Returning to consider once more Goldy's picture of the Western Pacific Ocean's spread-out map of the atolls and the water peoples' raft and outriggered sailing canoe coursings of those vast waters, first to reach eastward by rafts the Aleutians and the western shores of the Americas, secondly to reach westward to Oriental, Australian, Arabian, and African mainlands. This picture embraces the domain of 54 percent of all humanity (two billion people in 1975). Unseen in the picture are Europe and Western Africa combinedly embracing 32 percent of humanity, while out of sight, halfway around the world from Goldy's picture, exist the remaining 12 percent of humanity dwelling in the combined Americas.

In this Pacific and Indian ocean seascape of Goldy's it is a fact of significance that throughout all the seascape area extending outwardly from mainland China, starting in Japan and fanning the Pacific Ocean southward to Burma, all the much-used basketry containers are woven with a three-way-interconvergent triangle and hexagon grid. In dramatic contradistinction, all the basketry of the rest of the world is woven with a two-way parallel warp-and-woof grid. The triangle is the distinguishing mark of the sailor who had to learn how to structure powerfully enough to cope with the frequent fury of the sea. The sailor had to learn how to triangularly stay his masts against the enormous wind loads and powerfully heaving motions of the sea. Also unique to this same South Pacific, China coast area is the fact that the foundations and roof contours of its buildings constitute arcs of circles that curve upward at their ends in reverse of the curvature of the earth, which up-ended curvature corresponds to their ships' keels whose long end arcs also curve upwardly—and which keels became the symbols of the ancient Japanese Shinto religion's keel-shaped, red-painted torii mounted spanningly between two high red columns. The torii mark the entrance to invisible, open space shrines of worship. They are installed in places where Nature's exceptional beauty fills the invisible cathedrals with the presence of God. The up-at-the-ends curving foundations of Austronesia and Indochina are clearly seen, for instance, in the temples of Cambodia or in the Imperial Palace at Bangkok.

In contradistinction, we find the foundations of the Mayan buildings of Yucatan to be line-of-sight straight—that is, straight lines tangent to the curvature of the earth. The straightness of these foundations was probably inherited from the straight log lines of the great rafts by which these people first came after months of voyaging from Austronesia to Central and South America.

The raft people thought realistically of their straight-line raft as a plane, tangential to the great sphericity of their for-millions-of-years-observed, circular oceanic horizon and its ever-present spherical hilltop effect, which caused the tops of all objects going away or being left behind and beyond the horizon in any direction to perceptibly and progressively lower and finally disappear altogether, as Goldy has already pointed out but considers well worth repeating. If your vessel or raft kept moving day after day and month after month over the ocean surfaces and the spherical hilltop condition persisted, you might very logically come to think that you were traveling around the surface of a sphere, a very common shape. What is identified in the British Museum as "the first known 'toy' of humanity" is a six-inch-diameter ball, three-way-woven of split bamboo, first found in Burma and as yet used there instead of a pneumatic ball in a rugbylike game. The bamboo ball has a bounce and resilience equal to that of pneumatic ones.

Viewing the foundation lines of the great Greek and Roman temples such as the foundations of the Parthenon on the Acropolis, or of any of the great historical European structures, it will be seen that they too are curved, but oppositely to the foundations of the maritime Orient. The

Greek and "Near East" foundation curvature exactly follows that of the earth's surface. Their ends curve smoothly in constant congruence with the earth's circumference arc. Having been produced with plumb-bobs, the Greeks' successive columns of marble were supposed to be parallel to one another. Successive verticality assumedly produced parallel lines in the ken of the greater Mediterranean theater of yesterday's history. They assumed a flat-plane world, all the perpendiculars to which must be parallel to one another.

However, the blond-haired Dorian Greeks came into the Peloponnesos from the north, and it is probable that their building crafts emanated from their long earlier, ribbed-and-thronged-together, and subsequently seam-pitched, thwart-seated rowing boats of their blond-haired Viking ancestors, who when they reached the Baltic and Scandinavian coasts beached and overturned their boats to provide a roof for their winter homes. This overturning reversed the sky-pointing bow and stern curvature to an earthward-pointing curvature coincident with the earth's curvature. With that concept conditioning the Dorians would spontaneously accept the Greeks' earth congruent foundation curvature without any further reasoning.

Their Viking ancestors had often clustered four of their upside-down boats together end to end in the form of a cross, which originally brought about the naming of the great chamber of the later centuries' cathedrals. This chamber, which was situated below the great cruciform intersection of those cathedrals' stone-ribbed ceilings, became known as the "nave"—the boat. This boat-originated overturning reversed the boat's keel-line curvature of Oriental building. Most of Austronesia was tropical. There were no snow loads to be supported on roofs. The beached boats were not overturned. People slept outdoors or in leaf- and bamboo-contrived huts. The Japanese also had reached far enough northwardly in the Pacific to have to cope with winter, as had the Vikings in the Atlantic Arctic. The Japanese name for the "roof" and the inside of that roof is the same word as that meaning "bottom of the boat." The keels of the Vikings and Japanese acted as the ridge poles of their buildings.

Thinking in terms of the Greek actors' masks, Goldy identifies the down-ended foundation lines' curvature of the Near East, Mediterranean, and European worlds with the downwardly curved mouth ends of the mask of dismay and grief; she identifies the flat-out, straight-line Central American Mayan foundations with the tight and straight lips of scientific determination; and the upwardly curved foundation lines of the oceanic Orient she identifies with the upwardly curved mouth of placid good humor.

Goldy and the bears now discuss the fact that when the atoll-incubated humans first began to penetrate the mainland, they dug vast systems of canals into the shorelands to extend and complement their normal sea life support with additional life support grown in the freshwater-fed fields and paddies lying adjacent to their saltwater canals, which latter served to float their life-support boat cargoes to their floating water markets. Their half-water, half-land life gave these oceanic people the opportunity of capturing, taming, and domesticating both animals and vegetation by inbreeding them for emphasis of desired life-support characteristics. Thus developed the earliest, primarily waterborne, canal states which were ruled by kings who were, by demonstrated facts, the most physically capable of protecting their kingdoms against invaders. Because no one knew why the physically big and strong ones happened to be born big and powerful, the legend readily developed that the kings were divinely selected—ergo, were living demigods.

Goldy now draws a picture of what is often mistakenly spoken of by twentieth-century European and American tourists as a "temple." Goldy says, however, that these local demi-universe models were only to serve the monarch at the time of his death—as a great "step" ladder into heaven their cosmological model started with a large watery lake surrounding the miniature world. Centrally within this lake the god of the sea, Naga, sculptured in stone, completely surrounded the perimeter of their square, islanded world. Angkor Wat in Cambodia is the best remaining example of these cosmological models. It is completely surrounded by a square body of water which long ago led off by canals to the sea.

STONE 12

Goldy and the bears take note that there is one other important and sweeping difference between these water people of Austronesia and the rest of the world's land-conditioned people. This difference was discovered by a lifelong student of these people named Austin Coates, who found that none of the water and islands people in Goldy's oceanic Orient picture understands or wants to understand the land people's game called "business." As a consequence, four Chinese merchant families run all the business of Indonesia's 124 million people dwelling on 13,000 islands with 1,500 people per square mile concentrated on the island of Java. These water people can understand trading but cannot comprehend "credit" and the latter's anticipated or delayed balancing of economic events. They know that they cannot accredit wind for their sails in advance of the arrival of Nature's wind. And when the wind comes into their sails, they are confident that they do not owe anybody anything for it. They can only comprehend the reality of dealing directly with Nature and her unique energetic behaviors, as matter or radiation. They know that the wind from the banker's lungs will get the sailor nowhere. All the water people are committed to cooperatively producing life-support items such as foods, tools, and music. They march together single file out to the rice paddies and back—they sing together, dance together, make masks and costumes and act plays together. They cannot accredit as reality any of the middleman's tricks for cutting himself in on the life-support wealth of which the businessman has produced nothing. The latter "cuts" himself "in" only by building "walls," both physical and abstract, around the goods and service exchanges, control of the portals of whose abstract, or physical, walls permits the businessmen to produce false scarcities and elevated prices. The business banker also maneuvers himself into a position of politically profitable power by extending credit at interest to one while withholding it from others.

The water people have been educated both by Nature's intense, high-frequency, hostile environment events at the interface of the water and air ocean worlds, as well as by Nature's most benign and divine environment contriving. The water people know humans can't bluff the ocean, and they don't try. They know a vast stone fortress is defensively formidable but objectively useless: it can't float or transport you anywhere. The symbolic security and implied power of the banker's bank building does not inspire sea people's respect. To them, business is clearly intent upon self-advantaging at the expense of the many. "Since business is alien to the sea people," says Goldy, "we can find the origins of business only on the dry land, where long long ago a few physically powerful individuals mounted horses and rode up to a lonely shepherd tending a great flock of sheep in the wilderness grazing lands. Their leader said, 'Mr. Shepherd, that's too valuable a flock of sheep to be wandering unprotected in the wilderness. You need protection!' To which the shepherd replied, 'I do not: I and my sheep are never molested out here. There is no one to molest us.' Next morning the shepherd finds some of his flock have been killed. Around comes the armed man of the horse and says, 'Oh, what a pity. I told you that you needed protection, and you paid no attention to my friendly and experienced advice.' "

After a few more such repeated losses the shepherds or the cowherds of the goods-transporting caravans yield and accept the overlordship protection of the horse-mounted strongman and his gangland henchmen. The invisible walls and doors have been built. Once established, the power structure needed "brains" to help keep the conquered divided and thereby conquered and to keep productivity controlled in ways which most successfully syphoned the potential wealth advantage into the power structure's account by taking the people's deposited wealth, making loans, charging interest, collecting taxes, making laws, holding courts of judgment. The power structure also conscripted and armed fighting men to maintain their physical power, whose strength of numbers they always kept at the highest level consistent with maintaining the greatest possible gross overall productivity of the real life support and wealth.

Goldy says that true life-support wealth is produced not only by cultivation and harvesting but by adding value to matter by shaping it into needed tools such as levers and operating those tools with the natural energy income. Real wealth is also produced by completely employed technology whenever and wherever it effects: (a) reduction of customarily accepted spoilage, and (b) increase in longevity of storability or (c) increase in range and speed of life-support deliverability so that it may reach and advantage ever more people in ever more efficient and in ever higher quality manner, (d) increase in energy-use efficiency through using the best of several design alternatives (for instance, reciprocating engines have an efficiency of fifteen percent; turbines thirty percent; jets sixty percent; fuel cells eighty percent—ergo, by employing the technology that produces the greatest percentage of effective energy work accomplished), (e) continual reclaiming, sorting, recycling, and reusing the chemical element resources, (f) proliferation of technical know-how amongst all humans.

Goldy also tells the bears that she does not think of the business people or any other people as "bad." She says she realizes that the development of the lives of all humans is powerfully controlled by the special circumstances of each life. The bears concur: "From here we can see that all humans are very innocent participants in an evolving life process whose significance could not be made apparent or discovered until an enormous amassment of experience, which was and is as yet to be tested only through myriads of trials and errors."

Unlike the cow- and sheepherds, the sea people had no "flocks of fish" to guard, and the sea was as rough on the pirates as it was on the cargo carriers, whose ships if well designed and built could outmaneuver the pirates even when the latter improved their armament, for the cargo carriers could also improve their armament. In the end, however, the land lords extended their power out onto the sea to control the whole world and did so by controlling the credit system that underwrote the ventures and also by controlling the media of import/export exchanging and by building governments and the latters' great navies of invincible fighting ships, supported by fleets of supply ships, world-around naval bases, prime harborside supply sources, and by the ownership of minings, refining, and manufacturing processes.

While there is in reality only one world ocean which surrounds and separates all the islands and continents of the planet earth, and while it is true that the most physically powerful seacraft masters have gradually developed so many tricks for usurping the life-support productivity of the many for the exclusive benefit of the few, it is also probable that the millions of years of intimate experience with nature of the Austronesian water people, cannot and probably never will be willing to corrupt the logic of their reality in order to accommodate and accept the ninety-nine-percent fictitious credit bluffing game of the businessones. The Austronesians can fearlessly ride a twenty foot-high breaking wave in from the sea to safety on the beach and know that the bluffers perish.

Goldy and the bears now discuss the fact that when the atoll-incubated humans first began to penetrate the mainland, they dug vast systems of canals into the shorelands to extend and complement their normal sea life support with additional life support grown in the freshwater-fed fields and paddies lying adjacent to their saltwater canals, which later served to float their life-support boat cargoes to their floating markets. Their half-water, half-land life gave these oceanic people the opportunity of capturing, taming, and domesticating both animals and vegetation by inbreeding them for emphasis of desired life-support characteristics. Thus developed the earliest, primarily waterborne, canal states which were ruled by kings who were, by

76

demonstrated facts, the most physically capable of protecting their kingdoms against invaders. Because no one knew why the physically big and strong ones happened to be born big and powerful, the legend readily developed that the kings were divinely selected—ergo, were living demigods selected by the great gods, who obviously visited humans by sea and sky, being manifest as lightning, thunder, and storms as well as by bounteous life support—when the gods were pleased—and by disasters—when they were wrathful. The ruler had his people build for him a miniature world upon which at death the ruler might ascend to his throne amongst the other gods.

Goldy now draws a picture of what is often mistakenly spoken of by twentieth-century European and American tourists as a "temple." Goldy says, however, that these local demi-universe models were only to serve the monarch at the time of his death—as a great "step"ladder into heaven—allowing the dead ruler to physically ascend the heights to enter the universe of the gods. These cosmological models formalized in miniature humanity's concept of the Universe. Anyone who had traveled knew, said the Austronesians, that in due course you would come to the sea: obviously the sea surrounds everything. Therefore, their cosmological model started with a large watery lake surrounding the miniature world. Centrally within this lake the god of the sea, Naga, sculptured in stone, completely surrounded the perimeter of their square, islanded world. Angkor Wat in Cambodia is the best remaining example of these cosmological models. It is completely surrounded by a square body of water which long ago led off by canals to the sea. The way in which the canals led off to the sea and once completely gridded the lowland country is clearly visible in the land and water form pattern as seen from an airplane today.

The surrounding porticos of their great cosmological models were first produced with their upside-down wooden-ribbed boats, which wood-ribbed sheds were later replaced by stone structuring fashioned to emulate the earlier wooden-ribbed prototypes. They designed these great cosmological structures with the square base of their ocean rafts and oriented them to north, south, east, and west facings. Their model gave rise to the old expression, "the four corners of the earth." In their time it was thought that anybody who traveled knew that as you went inland on an atoll or on the mainland, you always came to ever higher mountains, and the higher one could climb on the inland mountains, the closer did they approach the dominion of the gods. But such climbing was only for the demigod king and only to be undertaken by him at the time of his death.

TRICAP 13

Atoll humans quickly learned that wood floats and stones sink. They learned that a single floating log rolls and that two floating logs held cross-connected by their branches do not roll, but provide a structurally stable floating device from which they could fish or dive for edible mollusks. The atoll dwellers soon learned to build both multilogged rafts and dugout log boats as well as outrigger-stabilized dugout canoes. Then they learned how to stitch together the palm tree's fronds to make combined masts and sails and found that their outrigger canoes could sail zigzaggingly to windward while rafts could only ride with the ocean currents or drift to leeward with the wind. The outrigger canoes could be worked (or could "beat") to windward by a succession of individual "tackings," first leftward, then rightward, at a firmly sail-filling angle, which is about thirty degrees one side or the other of the direction from which the wind is coming. This produced a low atmospheric pressure on the forward and leeward side of their sails, which, as with twentieth-century airplane wingfoils, pulled their boats forward in the direction of least resistance, which direction could be modifyingly controlled by steering oars or paddles. The atoll sailors, facing forwardly in their much-earlier-developed, large, dugout, outrigger canoes, learned to paddle them into the wind to become, undoubtedly, the first successful westward sea travelers against the prevailing winds. But this windward travel against the waves took both musclepower and much food to support it, which curtailed the length of voyaging. Nonetheless, it did make possible for the first time in history the predetermined (and celestial-navigation-maintained) direction of travel independent of the direction winds of and ocean currents, team paddling powered their voyages of discovery around islands, along seacoasts, and inland to explore the rivers. It established the principal mode of travel of the canaled, water-state kings of those four-cornered cosmological models (of kingly ascent into the realm of the gods).

STONE 13

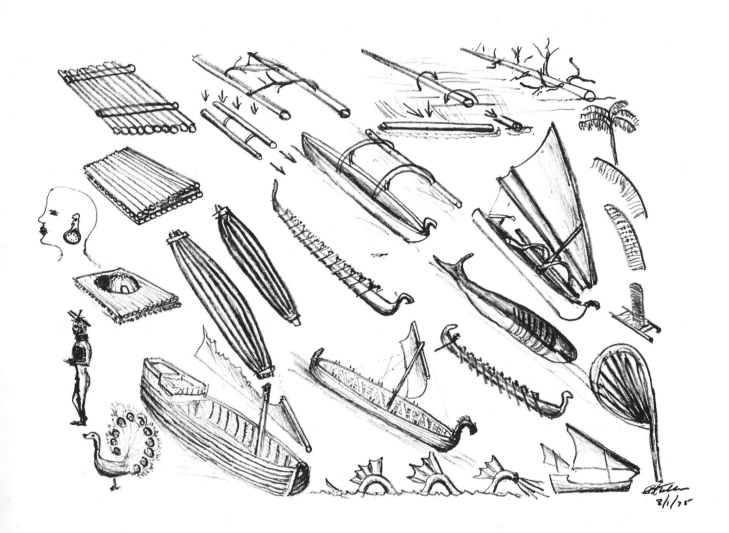

The bears tell Goldy that they had witnessed the early, large-rafting, Pacific water people going from the Pacific into the Atlantic, thence into the Indian and back again into the Pacific, blown dominantly west to east by winds, waves, and currents of the "roaring south latitude forties" not-so-merrily-go-rounding south of Capes Horn, Hope and South Island of New Zealand. This South Pole encircling confirmed to these water people incredible millennia ago that their world is a sphere—a spherical vessel going around the sun.

Their little independent world—their vessel seemed also to define a sphere of their locally controlled activity, within which spherical vessel (like the moon) they were encircling the larger world.

Undoubtedly endowed with same brains and minds as present-day humans—but naked, pocketless, and ofttimes drenched by overbreaking seas—these raft voyagers spent millions of long, clear-skied nights of their untold millennia to millions of sea travel years studying the familiar, nightly repeated view of their remote starry sky patterns as their spherical world rotated around its North Star and Southern Cross axis. They learned how the angular directions of these nightly viewed patterns gradually changed with their travel to disclose old or new star guides. As they went north, "the Southern Cross" became lost to sight and the North Pole star appeared ever higher above their horizon, and as they went south the pole star gradually became lost to view while "the Cross" became ever more elevatedly prominent, There being an equatorial area from which both the North Pole star and the South Pole's cross could be mutually but only vaguely viewed because of their proximities to the diametrically opposite horizon points.

Having no paper or writing tools with which to record their discoveries, the raft sailors lashed together complex, crisscrossed bamboo stick grids which faithfully corresponded with the sighted angles at different times when held aloft to their eyes to sight the interstar patterns. Thus the water people's rafts became the world's first "observatories" and these voyagers the first great astronomers, oceanographers, and mathematicians. As ocean currents and trade winds periodically reversed their drifting, they reconfirmed those seafarers' earlier powerfully remembered, stick-codified sightings.

During all their long years of voyaging, having no written means of amassing records of their experiences, they composed songs which, of very many verses, chronicled not only their own experiences but also those relayingly learned from the many generations of their ancestors, through the overlapping of their lives, who, too, had progressively amassed the records of their sea-voyaging experiences in chants. The Naga chants became the Ragas of the Japanese or Balinese, meaning "the tales of the old people" or the sagas of the Vikings. They were re-hearsed day after day, year after year, century after century by these long voyagers who kept track of the verses by successive identification of the verses with their succession of ancestors, each identified with a successive log in their rafts. Later each rib in their boats was identified with the successively chanted-of ancestor. When these people came later to turn their boats upside down on the land to protect the voyagers from the inclement weather, they gradually developed therefrom ribbed, roofed, and columned buildings for nonseagoing communal purposes. Thereafter they carved faces, arms, and legs on the columns and affixed small mother-of-pearl shell "eyes" on these faces, to represent the succession of earlier ancestors, and sung their chants before them.

However, long before those ribs appeared in the boats, the atoll sailors, facing forwardly in their much-earlier-developed, large, dugout, outrigger canoes, learned to paddle them into the wind to become, undoubtedly, the first successful westward sea travelers against the prevailing winds. But this windward travel against the waves took both musclepower and much food to support it, which curtailed the length of voyaging. Nonetheless, it did make possible for the first time in history the predetermined (and celestial-navigation-maintained) direction of travel independent of the direction of winds and ocean currents. Team paddling powered their voyages of discovery around islands, along sea coasts, and inland to explore the rivers. It established the principal mode of travel of the canaled, water-state kings of those four-cornered cosmological models (of kingly ascent into the realm of the gods).

TRICAP 14

Thus the human sailormen worked ever westward and ever farther off shore until in the lower latitudes of the Indian Ocean their westwardly headed voyaging was reversed by the powerful, eastwardly flowing Antarctic's world whirlaround of wind and water. Six thousand miles south of, unbeknownst to any other, terrestrial humans this eastward world whirlaround distributed those voyagers into the Pacific, Atlantic, and Indian oceans. Many of those sailors not washed overboard from their craft and drowned were wrecked and marooned on the myriad of lonely, barren islands scattered widely apart in the world's southern seas. Thus we find waterborne humanity first paddling, then rowing, then sailing determinedly westward into the wind to follow the life-giving sun's sky course, gradually working farther off shore and at their southern extremes of voyaging being unexpectedly caught in and swept along by the world-around eastward forces to bring about human occupation of many of the very remote islands of our planet.

Those voyagers marooned on lonely islands who found the food, water, and sheltering means to survive became scavengers of subsequent shipwrecks on the treacherous rocks of those islands. Hundreds and even thousands of generations of remote inbreeding developed highly differentiated physical and cultural features.

The historically unprecedented swiftness of twentieth-century development of the world-around integrating transportation and communication means is now trending to rapidly integrate and cross-breed back to an average world-human all these isolated increments of humanity of the islands as well as of those inbred among isolated inland tribes. In this way ever-evolutionary Universe has contrived first to conserve by isolation all the lessons learned regarding humanity's artifact-inventing ingenuity in coping with the most extreme conditions experienced around our planet and secondly to synergetically integrate all knowledge for the mutual advantage of all humanity.

STONE 14

Such paddled barges of royalty are as yet employed on state occasions by the king of Thailand and for many years were also so paraded annually by the great doges of Venice, clearly indicating the long-ago westward-reaching travel of these into-the-wind team paddlers. Later, standing and facing forward, the water people began also to use their steering oars mounted in oarlocks to propel them forwardly, as in the sampans of Thailand (and later gondolas of Venice), and thus developed the practical use of the lever in boat propulsion. This leverage advantage was not developed in full effectiveness until humans had crossed the Indian and Arabian seas in their sailing dugouts and in their four-of-five, bent-together-at-their-two-ends log rafts and sailing boats such as are as yet in use in southern India. After the sailors had reached northeastern Africa and had crossed overland from the Red Sea to the navigable waters of the Nile, most probably at the point where the Egyptian capital of Luxor developed, they flow-floated via the Nile northward to the Mediterranean. The trans-Indian Ocean sailors also sailed northward in the Red Sea to its two northern extremities, Aqaba and Suez, and went overland to build their boats anew in the Nile delta and along the Levantine coast of the Mediterranean. Others paddled their great, seagoing, ribbed canoes along the shores of India and Persia, to reach the Gulf of Oman and the Persian Gulf and thereby Mesopotamia, and at the headwaters of the Tigris and Euphrates rivers, ever following the sun, they caravaned overland through what became Damascus to reach the Mediterranean.

The multi-oared boat with oarsmen facing aft and only the steering-oar helmsman facing forward seems to have been a simultaneous invention by all these water people, all occurring in the Near and Middle East. They appear simultaneously in the Nile, Mediterranean, Indian Ocean, and Greece and were probably the principal vessels of Crete, thereafter rowing as well as sailing, developed to powerful degree with banks of slaves as the power source of the watercraft. With their new rowing capability humans coasted westward and out through Gibraltar, then northward along the coast of Europe—finally reaching and rounding Scandinavia's North Cape to reach the Arctic shores of Finland and Russia.

Goldy and the bears find the "sun boat" of the Egyptian pharaoh and the Vikings' long boat dug out of the mud at Oslo, and the Phoenicians' around-Africa and later across-both-the-Atlantic-and-Pacific voyaging craft, to be the same design—multiribbed, thonged-together, lap-straked, pitched seam, cross-thwarted, single bank, multi-oared rowing boat with a small, demountable, central mast and square, "with-the-wind" sail—and find that historic Oslo-

Viking boat's complicatedly carved Naga figurehead to be the same as one other only such known carved head in the world, which was found in the funeral-boat cave in North Borneo, indicating that the bull-horn headdress of the Vikings and the bull-horn symbol of the Cretans and the horse figurehead of the Phoenicians and Venetians are all symbols of the same sailormen, making it also clear that the powerfully rowed deep sea craft, in which horned cattle and horses were first carried as the trading money, were the same craft with which the Crete-Babylon axis plied their trade all the way east to Borneo and all the way westward and northward to the northwest coasts of Europe and the Americas. These hardy water people's Arctic-Sea-reaching Vikings became the founders of Russia and went thereafter southward overland to the headwaters of the Volga, thence by boats again southward, returning to the Mediterranean via the Caspian and overland again to the Black, Bosphorus, and Aegean seas. With each experience-informed design advance and enlargement of the powerful, ribbed ships of the Viking-Phoenician type, the ever deeper south in the Indian Ocean and along the southern coast of Africa did their voyaging take them.

Thus the human sailormen worked ever westward and ever farther off shore until in the lower latitudes of the Indian Ocean their westwardly headed voyaging was reversed by the powerful, eastwardly flowing Antarctic's world whirlaround of wind and water. Six thousand miles south of, and unbeknownst to any other terrestrial humans, this eastward world whirlaround distributed those voyagers into the Pacific, Atlantic, and Indian oceans. Many of those sailors not washed overboard from their craft and drowned were wrecked and marooned on the myriad of lonely, barren islands scattered widely apart in the world's southern seas. Thus we find waterborne humanity first paddling, then rowing, then sailing determinedly westward into the wind to follow the life-giving sun's sky course, gradually working farther off shore and at their southern extremes of voyaging being unexpectedly caught in and swept along by the world-around eastward forces to bring about human occupation of many of the very remote islands of our planet.

Those voyagers marooned on lonely islands who found the food, water, and sheltering means to survive became scavengers of subsequent shipwrecks on the treacherous rocks of those islands. Hundreds and even thousands of generations of remote inbreeding developed highly differentiated physical and cultural features.

The historically unprecedented swiftness of twentieth-century development of the world-around integrating transportation and communication means is now trending to rapidly integrate and cross-breed back to an average-world human all these isolated increments of humanity of the islands as well as of those inbred among isolated inland tribes. In this way ever-evolutionary Universe has contrived first to conserve by isolation all the lessons learned regarding humanity's artifact-inventing ingenuity in coping with the most extreme conditions experienced around our planet and secondly to synergetically integrate all knowledge for the mutual advantage of all humanity.

A major portion of the great historical heritage emanates from these first atoll-incubated humans. In addition to Goldy's discovery of the commonality amongst the Pacific water people of—(1) three-way basketry and other triangular structural weaving, (2) their upswept architectural foundations and roof-lines, (3) their total inability to accredit "credit" and to conduct business in the land-founded "Western" way—Goldy observes four other common characteristics of her water-world people: (4) their common Polynesian language base, covering an area one-quarter of earth's surface (which is in marked contrast to the diverse multiplicity of the language bases of the mainland peoples of earth, which often change every few miles, (5) the commonality of the binomial mathematical base of the Polynesians, (6) the commonality of their spontaneous unalterable omni-world, omni-motion, omni-equi-advantaging world community viewpoint and initiative, and (7) their omni-conviction that the physical organic body is not life, that life is abstract, weightless, immortal. The water people's funeral pyres are celebrations of happiness.

Goldy says to the bears, "Your thought-communicated knowledge guided me intuitively as I speculated my way through that early history, and I am grateful." So—here we go again—having jumped from the Arabian into the eastern Mediterranean, where we come to the 1400 B.C. palace at Knossos on Crete, where we find the sign of the king carved into the stone walls of his chambers. The king's sign is a hexagon enclosing a set of six equilateral triangles surrounding a central point arranged in six sixty-degree angular increments. Contrasting with this king's symbol we find in the household area of the palace the distaff symbol carved into the walls. The "distaff" is a square enclosing two crosses—the perpendicular and the diagonal. It resembles the British flag divided centrally into ninety-degree and forty-five-degree angles.

The Cretan water king's symbol is that of the three-way Oriental water people's triangular basketry weaving and triangular celestial navigation, while the distaff symbol of the land people's area is the two-way square-weaving symbol of the world's dry-land "square"-dealing civilizations.

As carved into the king's wall, one of the six points of the hexagon is topmost, another bottommost. The almost exclusively land-minded archaeologists have misidentified this form with what they call the double or two-way axe head. They assumed the vertical axis of the hexagon to be the staff of the axe with two-way blades, one facing right, one facing left. However, it is more probable that the vertical axis hexagon of the Cretan king's wall symbol was an angularly formalized profile of a spherical earth, showing (A) its north-south polar axis and (B) its Arctic and Antarctic areas and also showing the earth's central angle between the Tropics of Cancer and Capricorn, between whose latitudes occurred the most propitious sailing and living conditions. Goldy says that with the first coinages of humanity now being brought out from Mediterranean ocean bottoms, one of the most frequent is that of the sailor's symbol—the double-headed, two-way-facing Janus whose overall contour is that of the king's symbol, the vertical axis hexagon. Dry-land anthropologists and archaeologists have ministerpreted the Janus symbol as meaning only that the sailor was a notorious liar, professing to be going one way but actually going the other. To the maritime archaeologists and anthropologists the Janus symbol clearly reveals that the sailors knew that they could face in any direction and, traveling constantly in that great-circle direction, come back to where they started because the earth is a sphere.

The Three Bears say that this latter knowledgeable interpretation of Goldy's is powerfully fortified by the forehead-crowning symbol the Egyptian navigator priests always gave to their land-preoccupied pharaohs. This crowning symbol consists of the sea god, Naga, the sea serpent, rising two ways around an orb to join together at its top. This either-way-around-the-world voyaging symbol was never understood by the land-preoccupied pharaohs. For thousands of years the navigator-'astronomer-' mathematician-priests successfully monopolized the secret knowledge of the earth's sphericity and of its faraway, fabulous life-support resources as well as of startlingly unfamiliar mineral, metallic, and other herb resources, which resources were exclusively reachable "overseas" only by the priest-navigators. But either the navigator-priests or the Phoenicians left their traditional symbol in Central America in a number of pottery spheres entirely around whose spherical surfaces the Nagas (serpents) wind.

The bears tell Goldy that these navigator-priests were the ones who had secreted to their own advantage the ancient knowledge of yin-yang etcetera. The bears then tell Goldy that they had witnessed with interest how the navigator-priests' capability had inadvertently evolved into a "miracle" resource only infrequently employed by atoll, islander, and mainland chieftains and monarchs when those supposedly divinely ordained leaders found the tribal credit for their kingly wisdom as a lawmaker, judge, or fighter to be deteriorating. They knew that all they had to do was to ask their navigator-priests for a miracle, which the navigator always was able to produce for them in the form of any object completely unfamiliar to his people because it was non-occurrent in his islanded kingdom, having been brought from other distant, ocean-intervened lands.

The kings knew nothing of navigation or of the foreign lands. They had no idea how the navigator-priest obtained the miracle. All they knew was that the priest-navigator could always produce a never-before-seen item with which they could confront their people, the obvious strangeness of which object restored their people's superstitious belief in the divine origin and continuing divinely administered wisdom of their leader. Navigation of the intuitively sensitive, complex integration and calculation, carried on entirely in their heads and requiring lifelong experience and courage to sail away out of sight of any land for days, moving toward an invisible destination, was not an art that could be stolen from them and was one they imparted only to their own sons or adopted sons. This put the navigator-priest in an utterly mysterious and privileged category throughout all the past history of humans. He is the "Merlin" of the King Arthur legend's court, which evolved in the dim past of those all-European, harbor-commanding, Anglo-Saxon islands, which were reached at least 3,500 years ago by the westwardly rowing Phoenicians and Vikings, which date is attested to by the 1500 B.C., uniquely Mycenaean type of gold breastplate and sword found buried in the ground at Stonehenge.

The great empires of Mesopotamia and Egypt saw these navigator-priests, in a long succession of their profession from its origin in Austronesian atolls, from time to time coming out upon the ever-westwardly attained lands to secretly control the local kings and thereby secretly to manipulate for better or for worse the societies of those various lands. The priests' secrets were never in jeopardy of discovery by others when the navigators placed bejeweled gold orbs in the hands of the kings as symbols of their king's omni-sovereignty, knowing that the landlubber, flat-earth-fixated kings would not comprehend the sphere's significance as a model of the spherical world. The kings were aware only of their flatly mapped, local, dry-land domains.

Ever pioneering northwestward into the wind, following the life-giving sun, the navigator-priests came all the way from Austronesia, the Indian Ocean, and Arabian Sea, crossing overland northwestward into the Mediterranean Sea and its Aegean, Ionian, Adriatic, and Tyrrhenian sea components. The historically great power of three-and-one-half-millennia-ago Crete was the supreme power of the navigator-priest exercised over the king. As with the two-millennia-later Venice, Crete had no need for fortifications because at its time, together with its Indian-Ocean-traffic-mastering, Babylonian colleague, it ruled supremely over all the surrounding seas and all the water-borne lines of intersupply existing between all the people and all their far-flung life-support resources. The waters of spherical earth constitute one continuous ocean; the lands are isolated. Water people are world people. The sailor's symbol was the six-triangle hexagon, for only triangles are structurally stable. With their keeled, triangularly trussed framing and triangularly rigged ships, sailor-navigators have encircled the spherical earth. Land people have been historically local and ignorantly subservient to the earth's sphericity, commencing their wall buildings with stone, the land-holding and -guarding people build compressively, squarely, redundantly, and heavily. Commencing their shipbuilding with wood, water people build tensively, curvilinearly, triangularly, and with utmost efficiency of realized function per each ounce of weight, minute of time, and erg of energy designedly invested in their "environment-controlling" vessels. They must do ever more with ever less in order to float controllably in any manner of storms, while doing so much with so relatively little.

TRICAP 15

Traveling ever farther westward against the prevailing winds seemed to say that merchants and those who patronized them were deliberately contradicting the winds of God's will. This sailor-popularized apprehension greatly frustrated realization of the vast wealth potential in the east-west high-seas trade. For the miracle answer the kings, nobles, and merchants of Mesopotamia turned to the navigator-astronomer-priests of Babylon. To convince everyone in the new western world that accounts of any earlier religions or people elsewhere on earth were false, the priests said that the beginnings of humans in Universe had occurred nearby to Babylon in a garden called Eden. Their story from then on is well known. What seems pure nonsense in the Garden of Eden story of the creation of a woman from a man's rib is explained as follows. Vessels of the sea are always female because they contain their crews in their interior wombs. The female "Eve" was the high-seas, world-around-sailable vessel; her great strength developed when navigators discovered the backbone-mounted rib cage employed by Nature in the design of whales, porpoises, seals and other sea creatures. So man built his high-seas vessel, "Eve," with strong wooden ribs rising sidewise from her keel, planked "her" in, then leather-thong-fastened the planks' edges together, tied them tightly into the ribs, and pitched her seams. Thus "Eve" the ship, built from Adam's rib cage design, was temptingly "led on" by Naga the serpent, god of the sea, around the world, with Adam aboard. Thus Naga showed Adam, by means of Eve, that the earth is as round as the apple.

STONE 15

With the establishment of the Crete-Babylon navigator-priest axis came unified control of the sea-lane mastery of all the high-seas trade routes, eastward from the "Near East" to Malaysia and the Pacific via the Arabian Sea and Indian Ocean, and westward from the "Near East" to Europe via the Mediterranean and North Atlantic coast. Thus was established monopoly of a new and fabulously powerful "world" wealth growth, synergetically accruing to the exploitation of a vast variety of natural resources of our planet. A vast variety of human skills and an even vaster variety of human needs. The spices and herbs of the Orient rendered more palatable the swiftly decayable (uniced and unrefrigerated) foods of the Western World, while Oriental pitches made watertight the new ribbed and thonged-together ship's planking. The silks, precious stones, and metals brought powerful fortunes to those who possessed them. Ships can carry many-fold the cargoes transportable on the backs of animals or humans. So powerfully advantageous was the sea trade in these goods, and so much wealth could be had by bringing the gamut of remote resources to the ever newly colonizing Western World, that three great trade routes connecting the east and west ocean routes were established: (1) via East Africa's Somaliland to Egypt and the Nile, (2) via the Red Sea, and (3) via the Gulf of Persia, the Tigris and Euphrates, and thence caravaning overland to the easternmost coast of the Mediterranean.

Because the Nile always flowed northward and the winds always blew southward, the Nile became the easiest and most immediately profitable interconnection between the Indian Ocean and the Mediterranean Sea but involved a chain of human cargo bearers between the Nile's navigable headwaters and various routes to the Indian Ocean via Lake Victoria, etc. The Red Sea had one-way southwardly blowing winds but required paddling or rowing northward in lieu of long and laborious windward beating under sail, and since the rowing was much more effective, the Red Sea became the prime development waters of the Phoenicians' small, square-sail-rigged rowing craft. Route 3 via the Gulf of Persia, caravaning from Baghdad to Jericho to Damascus to Lebanon, was probably profitable in its own right because of the large market of customers along its inland route. What is now Somaliland was known in Egyptian times as the land of Pun. The word pun means red. The Red Sea was the Pun Sea—

the Sea of the Punicians—the Phoenicians. The waging of the Punic Wars against the Roman Empire was staged from Carthage on the North African coast. These "Puns" were the navigator pun-dits who invented their punts, i.e., their pole-pushed or single-oar-propelled boats—which punts later became the "ponts" of the pontoon bridge.

The westward paddling, rowing, sailing, was accomplished in a relatively short historical time span of approximately one millennium, compared to the possible millions of years of dominantly eastward Pacific raft driftings propelled only by prevailing winds and ocean currents, that it was popularly assumed such millennia of drifting ever yielded to God's will as expressed lucidly by the direction in which the winds and waters flowed. All humans had always assumed a benign omni-science and wisdom to be articulate in nature. The increasingly popular knowledge of humanity's ability to go successfully ever farther westward against the prevailing winds seemed to say that merchants and those who patronized them were deliberately contradicting the winds of God's will. This sailor-popularized apprehension greatly frustrated realization of the vast wealth potential in the east-west high-seas trade. The greater the sea trade, the larger grew the ship's crews. While sailors see a lot of water and sky, they don't know where they are at sea unless the captain or navigator tells them, and since they were never told where their ship might be at any given moment, and because the seas were frequently hostile, the sailors superstitiously interpreted the weather's behavior as being the disapproving voice of God. Because all the powerful chieftains and major monarchs greatly profited by westward trade, credit for the powerful leaders' wisdom in fostering the trade was deteriorating. Their power was threatened even more by the overland caravan trade from China, which was operating to the north in a relay system via the chain of inland seas and rivers. Caravaning could not carry the bulk and tonnage of the ocean vessels but could transport high-value, lightweight, and small bulk goods.

For the miracle answer the kings, nobles, and merchants of Mesopotamia turned to the navigator-astronomer-priests of Babylon, which was then the most central, population-wise, of their dilemma area. Probably conferring with their Egyptian and Cretan colleagues, the priests gave an answer that not only satisfied the popular need for a new philosophic explanation of what was transpiring in the world, but an answer that had several other effects beneficial to their particular monarchs and the latter's most favored traders. But it was also an answer designed to throw off course, off scent, and off trail the few individuals who were becoming too curious about the world-around trade routes' potentials and about the sources of the priests' "miracle objects," the knowledge of which the priests so carefully guarded. Conferring with their colleague chief priests of the Mediterranean and Arabian seas, it was agreed that above all the priests needed to convince everyone in the new Western World that accounts of any earlier religions of any other locals on earth were utterly false legends. Thus the priests said that the beginnings of humans in the Universe had occurred very nearby to Babylon in a garden called Eden. Their story from then on is well known. What they were covering up and needed to explain away were the sailors' tales that the navigator-priests had known for at least 10,000 years, that the earth is a sphere and that the water people had in fact been circumnavigating it for millennia. The sailors were also getting close to being able to explain how the priests obtained their miracles. These Sinbad-the-sailor tales were told in the seagoing terms of the sea people. Their rationalization of what seems pure nonsense in the Garden of Eden story of the creation of a woman from a man's rib is explained as follows.

Vessels of the sea are always female because they contain their crews in their interior wombs. The female "Eve" was in fact the high-seas, world-around-sailable vessel: "She" was capable of withstanding the great stresses of high-seas storms. This high-strength, multiribbed, big cargo-bellied vessel design was made possible when the navigators discovered the rib cage (analogous to that of humans) employed by Nature in the design of the backbone-mounted ribs of whales, porpoises, seals, walruses, and other large sea creatures, as well as noting the powerful structural stability attained in fishes by their longitudinal backbone and its sideways-arrayed rib bones. Clearly, man could produce a much more powerful and sturdy ship by employing this principle of a vertebral keel and its multirib structure to reinforce at right

94

angles his too flexible, longitudinally organized log-plank boats of Cape Comorin and of Trivandrum on the southwest coast and of Mahabalipuram on the southeast coast of India as the prototypes of the first break away from large, single-tree "dug-out" hulls switching over to larger vessels, which were multi-log-built vessels with powerfully lashed together ends fashioned of naturally grown, curved-trunk tree logs with pitch-filled seams—copied later in treeless Egypt with thong, bailed, or tied-together papyrus "logs" bound secondarily together in the same manner as the South India prototype. Their papyrus craft were similar to Thor Heyerdahl's twentieth-century "RA II"—which successfully sailed westward from Egypt out of the Mediterranean and across the Atlantic.

It was of course man's own rib cage that gave him a means of personally sensing the ribs' structural functioning. Just as human rib cages allowed humans great freedom of motion, such structure would allow the ship to "work" in the storm. So man, using the wood of the tree, built his high-seas vessel, "Eve," with strong wooden ribs mounted from its wooden keel, planked "her" (Eve) in, then leather-thong-fastened the planks' edges together and tied them tightly into the ribs. Thereafter they pitched her ("Eve's") seams. Thus prepared, "Eve" the ship, built from Adam's (lung-enclosing) rib cage design (this rib-born eve, deep-sea-capable "Eve") was temptingly led on by Naga the serpent, god of the sea. Eve followed Naga around the world with Adam aboard, and with this experience Naga (the sea serpent god of the sea) showed Adam, by means of Eve, that the earth is as round as the apple Naga had tempted her to realistically experience. The tree of knowledge was of course that possessed by the navigator-priest who had warned common humans not to try going too far in any direction lest they too discover that the earth is an apple and as such is a closed system, whereby if others went around it, the priests would have no more secret resources from which to produce their miracles. Big Bear says to Goldy, "Using one of your planet earth's expressions, 'you hit that one right on the nose.'"

TRICAP 16

When the blond-haired Vikings reached Scandinavia, they beached and overturned their large, powerfully keeled, transversely ribbed, thong-tied and pitch-seamed, longitudinally lap-straked boats to provide a watertight roof for their snow-covered winter homes. Mounting the boat ends on wooden "horses," the Vikings often clustered four boats end to end in the form of a cross and draped skirts of skins from the gunwales to the ground. This became the cruciform prototype of subsequent cathedrals, whose stone-ribbed ceilings' eaves (Eves) became known as the "nave"—the boat. Most of Austronesia was tropical. There were no snow loads to be supported. The beached boats were not overturned. The Japanese Austronesians also had reached far enough northward to have to cope with winter snows in the same manner as had the Vikings. The Japanese name for the house "roof" is the same as that meaning "bottom of the boat." During their long years of voyaging, having no written means of amassing records, the water people composed many verses chronicling their experiences and those learned relayingly from previous generations. The Naga chants became the ragas of the Japanese and Balinese, meaning "the tales of the old people" or the sagas of the Vikings. Rehearsed daily, millennium after millennium, successive verses were identified with successive ancestors and logs in their rafts or ribs in their boats. Later turning their boats upside down on the land to protect against the storms, they developed therefrom ribbed, roofed, and columned buildings for nonseagoing communal purposes, with the ancestors' features carved on their respective columns.

STONE 16

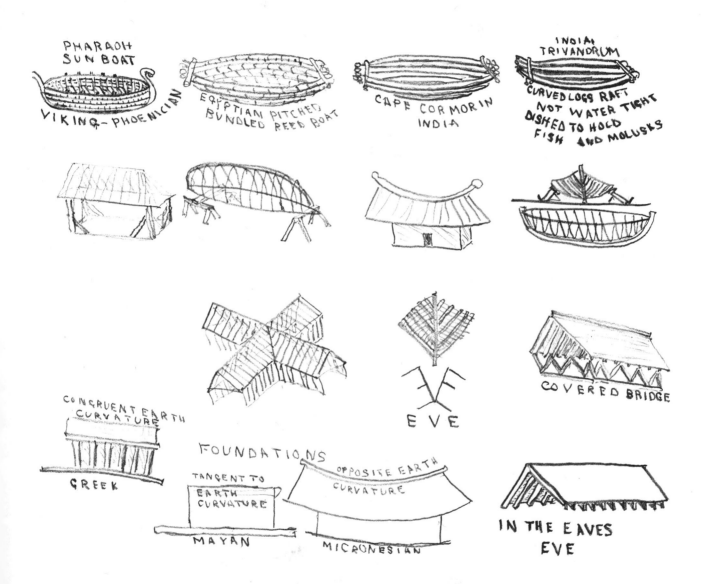

PHARAOH SUN BOAT
VIKING-PHOENICIAN

EGYPTIAN PITCHED BUNDLED REED BOAT

CAPE CORMORIN INDIA

INDIA TRIVANDRUM
CURVED LOGS RAFT
NOT WATER TIGHT
DISHED TO HOLD
FISH AND MOLUSKS

CONGRUENT EARTH CURVATURE
GREEK

FOUNDATIONS
TANGENT TO EARTH CURVATURE
MAYAN

OPPOSITE EARTH CURVATURE
MICRONESIAN

EVE

COVERED BRIDGE

IN THE EAVES
EVE

97

Goldy says that it is most probable that the westward-paddling, coastline-and-rivers-exploring, South Seas atolls people first landed on the mainland along the Malay Peninsula and the Indochina area, probably exploring the Mekong River as the first and largest of such great rivers nearest to the largest of the thousands of the Austronesian islands. The Mekong and other of the rivers they explored all led to the highland country northwest of the great Himalayan range in Tibet, whose eternal snow crown, melted by the southeast trade winds around its lower northwest slopes, shed their water eastward into the rivers of greater China as well as into India's Brahmaputra, Ganges, and Indus rivers, thus to water the lands from which has sprung the food to feed more than half of all humanity throughout all known history.

The first Austronesian China coast landing could have started four million years ago. Goldy goes on to recall how these newly landed Austronesians gradually domesticated the wild water buffalo, sheep, goats, elephants, camels, and horses. Of all the latter the horse was easiest to mount and the swiftest of travel. As the people gradually penetrated inland, first in the rivers and then along the river valleys, they domesticated their flocks and herds. Those traveling on horses far outsped and outdistanced the herders, who followed on foot the local to-and-fro grazing of their animals, which tended to remain in favorable localities. Unquestionably the horsemen and camelmen penetrated inland and explored farther and far earlier than any of the other humans, as all of them, fast or slow, steadily adapted themselves to the land life. As a consequence it is most probable that the horsemen, hindered by at least one Ice Age, staying south of the devastating winters of Siberia yet skirting north of the formidable Himalayas as they traveled ever westward across the Mongolian deserts and negotiable mountain passes of Asia, came to reach and ride along the shores or to raft over the waters of the succession of lakes and inland seas leading farther westward to the Aral, Caspian, Azov, and Black seas, thence using their long-earlier-acquired memory of boatbuilding to produce the water-link passaging boats and rafts. Finally they passed by water through the Hellespont to occupy the islands along the shores of the Aegean and Mediterranean seas, penetrating all the way to the Atlantic coast. There they lived hundreds of thousands of years ago primarily as horsemen, and during the last Ice Age developed and painted in caves and, millennia later, in the Stone Age. Riding over all the Eastern European and Middle East lands, they built forts in the lowlands and citadels in the mountains, hunting, ruling, and exploiting the herders and the fruit, nuts, leaves, and root gatherers, as Goldy previously described. The intervening long Ice Age accounts for the otherwise incredibly long hiatus between the first overland arrival in Western Europe of the original, Orient-landed, westwardly venturing Austronesians. The millennia-long and even millions of years of inbreeding, originally on thousands of different islands and subsequently in landlocked tribes, accounts for the vast differentiation in the physical aspects of these early human groups—the bleaching out of some, the darkening and ruddying of others.

TRICAP 17

The Austronesians caught and domesticated mainland animals millions of years ago. Their horsemen hunters penetrated inland earliest and fastest, reaching Europe, dwelling and painting in caves wherein they bleached out during the last Ice Age. In the subsequent Stone Age these horsemen built strategic citadels, exploited the herders and the fruit, nut, leaves, and root gatherers. Goldy now draws a map for the Three Bears showing the horsemen's multimillennia-earlier five east-to-west caravaning routes and how the evolving Indian Ocean ships could more swiftly carry much larger cargoes than caravans and how, despite the religiously biased way in which the priests and scribes chose to write Eurasian history, all of its military struggles were waged between empires secretly puppeted by the grand masters of the alternate east-west overland and water routes. Thus was Emperor Constantine puppeted into shifting Roman Empire headquarters to command the Bosphorus and reestablish the overland route. Seeking to reestablish the water route the "Holy Grail" drive of the "Crusaders" sought to wrest overland access to the Indian Ocean from the Moslem Saracens. After 4,000 years of struggling all Near-East-transiting trade was mothballed when Henry "The Navigator" of Portugal inaugurated sailing from Europe to the Orient via the Atlantic around Africa. Thereafter, a succession of world-ocean masteries culminated in the East India company's "British Empire"-puppeted supremacy over all the world's oceanic trade routes. This oceanic mastery suddenly terminated in World War II, when the line-of-supply control shifted into the air and is now shifting again into the airless ocean of outer nothingness, intervening relativity's cosmic events.

STONE 17

These horse and camel people became the first to travel back and forth along their most favorable routes between what became known in later European history as the Far East and the Near East. The Dravidian inhabitation of the southern coasts of India represented the second westward continental landing and settlement of the Austronesians, which settlements then served as basing points for much farther westward water venturing. The Luxor Egyptians constitute the second successful westward jump of waterborne civilization which maintained via East Africa its trade with the trans-Indian Ocean merchant ships. From the walls of the Egyptian navigator-priests' tombs we learn of their maritime technology history. So also from the walls of their Southern Europe caves we first learn of the Mediterranean presence of the millions-of-years-earlier-arrived horsemen hunters, who only 4,000 years ago came to invade the Egyptian Empire and its trans-Mesopotamian water world traders, whose presence appeared to the northern Mediterranean horsemen as a threat to their many-millennia-earlier monopolization by caravan of all the Far-East–Near-East trade. On the other hand the Egyptians considered themselves to be the most civilized of known people and technically very advanced because their Indian-Ocean-crossing ships could carry much larger cargoes than could be carried by human bearers or animals on the northerly overland routes and could cover the distance between the Far and Near East so much faster; the Egyptians looked upon the northern horsemen as hordes of wild barbarians. Obviously this provoked the northern "barbarian" horsemen, in this case the Hittites, into invading and eventually overwhelming the Egyptians. Thus began a series of historical strugglings of north vs. south—of the overland vs. waterborne east-west tradesmen. These wars were waged through their puppeteered monarchs and were always waged for some propaganda-invented "religious causes." Century after century, millennium after millennium, new great empires were established first by the power of the northern overlanders and next by that of the southern overseas, Orient-to-Europe exploiters. In the successively westward "nouveau riche" Near East and later European worlds the traders from the Orient "cashed in" on the thousands of years of earlier discovered and developed art, artifacts, and "riches" of Oriental civilization. The Mongol horsemen from the Black Sea and Caspian country rode south and west of the Himalayan range to invade India going eastward and northward along the Indus River and thence eastward again south of the Himalayas to cross the continental wastershed divide to reach the south and eastwardly flowing Ganges, along which they met the Austronesian water people who had traveled inland from the Bay of Bengal via the Ganges. The Mongol horsemen vanquished the on-foot, Indian-Ocean-landed Dravidians and founded the Mohenjo-Daro civilization.

Time after time the Mongol (Moguls) invaded India overland to completely master the lives of India's many-thousands- (possibly millions) -of-years-earlier-landed maritime coastal settlers, whose much earlier presence as yet remains to confound humanity by its two great (probably) Dravidian legacies—Mahabalipuram, meaning "the big Balinese (type) city" on India's southeast coast, and Elephanta on the northwest coast. Each of these are monolithic carvings reduced in place from one whole solid rock the size of a small mountain.

Elephanta, on an island in the harbor of Bombay, is a whole temple entered through an ornately sculptured rectilinear opening in the side of the mountaintop within which the interior of the mountain sculptured temple is complete with elegantly capped and pedestaled interior columns integral to the whole stone fashioning of the vast hand-sculpted cave temple, along each of whose interior walls are arranged heroic scale sculptures of the Vishnu-Siva-Brahma Trimurti (Trinity); while Mahabalipuram south of Madras on the east coast is one whole mountainous rock reduced in place to all the external surfaces of a monolithic temple surrounded by an array of the same monolithic carvings of life-size or heroic sculptures of realistically rendered elephants and other animals, while all the temple—its columns and interior sculptures of Vishnu-Siva, including much delicate and intricate roof-edge carving, including independent cut-stone chain links—is all integrally carved in place out of the one original solid-rock hill.

Mahabalipuram is an overall positive, convex, male conception, and Elephanta is a negative, concave, female enclosure conception with a positively sculptured interior. Despite hundreds of intervening miles Elephanta and Mahabalipuram are as inseparable—conceptually, philosophically, and stylistically—as are the coexisting concave and convex surfaces of a tennis ball. Most astonishing about these two, in contrast to the many later-era cave sculpturings of Buddhist monks in India, is that both Mahabalipuram and Elephanta appear to have been designed and executed by one sculptor in one day, so coherent and consistent is their rendering, whereas each must have taken hundreds if not thousands of years and many, many generations to accomplish. That so many people over so many generations could have seen so "eye to eye" with one another and maintained that comprehending coordination transcends any comprehension by humans of our era. It manifests how little change has taken place in millions of years in the way of the sea with humans and manifests the simple integrity of understanding of these half-a-planet-occupying Austronesian water people whose outrigger canoes sailed at twenty knots from their millions-of-years-ago inception—a speed never since exceeded by sailing craft—a people who speak only one basic language, who invented mathematics and the calculating machine, for the rings on their fingers, wrists, and necks were the forerunners of the abacus, the only kind of calculating machine suitable to a frequently wave- and rain-drenched naked people—who eons ago came out onto the subcontinent of India, Sri Lanka, and Madagascar from the smaller atolls of Austronesia just as they had somewhat earlier come out from the larger islands off the coast of Indochina and Malaysia, Java,

Sumatra, Burma, et al. This atoll-to-mainland transition covered millions of years and includes the three-and-one-half-million-years-ago Leakeys' humans, who landed on the northeast coast of Africa.

So much more powerful in combat on the land than the on-foot Austronesians were the horse-mounted Mongols who rode into northern India that they gradually pushed the Austronesian Dravidians into the southeast tongue of India and the present-day Sri Lanka.

Goldy now draws a map for the Three Bears showing the original most northerly route and its subsequently established competitors' alternate, overland, horsemen-blazed, caravan routes from China to the Mediterranean shores. Despite the biased way in which the priests and their scribes of the various empires chose to write history, practically all of its military struggles were waged through their puppet empires by the respective behind-the-scenes grand masters of commerce of the several successively o'erwhelming alternate overland and alternate water routes between the Orient and Occident. The succession of the all-Asia-Minor empires, starting with the Moguls' invasion of India and their founding of the Mohenjo-Duro period, went as follows: Chaldean, 3800 B.C.; Elamitic, 2000 B.C.; Egyptian, 1600 B.C.; Hittite, 1200 B.C.; Assyrian, 670–645 B.C.; Babylonian, 600 B.C.; Median, 600 B.C.; Persian, 500 B.C.; Greek Alexandrian, 323 B.C.; Roman 0–117 A.D.

Jerusalem (Urusalem) is situated approximately halfway between the dominantly northerly and the dominantly southerly routes and, in marked contrast to its name—Uru (city) Salem (peace)—has been successively captured and recaptured by the successive winners of the struggles for command of the wealth of exploitation in the west of the riches of the east, whose successive masters undertook to establish their own grandeur and augment their power by inventing the concept that the beginnings of human life occurred within their domains and when in combat with others proclaimed that they were the exclusive favorite of their one or more gods and that they had divine commission. The successive invisible grand masters of the ten east-west trade routes were the wealth-manipulating brains behind the successive empires encompassing all of Asia Minor. The ten successively dominant alternate east-west trade routes consisted of six which used rivers and lakes but were predominantly overland and four which crossed some dry land but were at least nine-tenths by water. All six of the overland routes went from Hankow on the Yangtse River, at whose mouth was Shanghai, and led from Hankow northwesterly to Lanchow, Kanchow, and Suchow to Sinkiang, whereafter they branched three ways, route 1 via Alma-Alta, the second route via Samarkand, and routes 3, 4, 5, and 6 via Kabul. Routes 1 and 2 run north of the Caspian into the Sea of Azov and there by water through the Bosphorus into the Aegean and Mediterranean seas.

104

Routes 3 and 4 ran from Sinkiang via the Khyber Pass and Kabul to skirt south of the Caspian and thereafter split into two more routes, one to the south shore of the Black Sea and thence to Tarsus on the northeastern corner of the Mediterranean, just northeast of Cyprus; while the other branched from the first where Tehran is now situated, ran southwest to the Euphrates, then northwest to Damascus and finally Tarsus. Routes 5 and 6 ran from Sinkiang through the Khyber Pass via Kashmir, whereafter route 5 ran via Babylon to Baghdad, Damascus, and Tarsus, and route 6 down the Indus River to where Karachi is now situated and thence overland to Babylon, Baghdad, Damascus, and Tarsus.

Route 7, the first of the four water routes from China and Indochina and India, was sailed and rowed via the Persian Gulf to Baghdad, thence up the Euphrates, thence overland to the Mediterranean. Route 8 ran via the Red Sea and Gulf of Aqaba to the Levantine coast, route 9 via the Red Sea to Suez and overland to the Nile delta, and route 10 via the Red Sea to a point closest to Luxor and overland to that early Egyptian capital, thence north on the Nile to the Mediterranean. Those ten routes resolve themselves into three most intercompetitive subgroups: the two northerly can be called the northerly group; the five routes all leading to Tarsus (four overland and one by water to Baghdad) can be called the middle group; and the three Red Sea routes can be called the early southerly group—but the route from the Red Sea to Gulf of Aqaba and thence overland to Jericho, Lebanon, and other Levantine coast ports forsook the southerly group and became a contestant for dominance of the middle group.

All of these early empires have their own complex of gods representing dominant attributes for life-giving, -managing, and -terminating functions. As with the early water people it was assumed that the gods were not concerned with the people but only with the temporal monarch, and that concern was only to secure the king a place among the gods. With a few millennia of development and proliferation of technological know-how, tools, physical materials, and building capability it was realized that in addition to equipping the monarch for safe passage into the afterlife, it would be feasible to assist all the nobles in safely reaching the next world, which was done by preparation of elaborate tombs in which were secreted all the riches, foods, and tools that the king (and later nobles) would need in the next life. As millennia passed so much know-how was accumulated that during the last millennium B.C. it became technologically feasible to prepare elaborate mausoleums to enable the rich middle class to migrate into the other world. Finally it became technically feasible to prepare all of humanity for entering into the afterlife. This occurred at year zero, when the southerly group came into command control of the east-west trade.

105

TRICAP 18

The Austronesians assumed that the gods were not concerned with the people but only with posthumous deifying of the king. With a few millennia of development and proliferation of technological know-how, tools, physical materials, and building capability, civilization realized that in addition to equipping the god-monarch for safe passage into the afterlife, it would be feasible also to assist the nobles to reach the next world. This was done by preparation of elaborate tombs in which were secreted all the riches, food and tools that the king (and later, nobles) would need in the next life. As millennia passed, so much know-how was accumulated in this life that during the last millennium B.C. it became technologically feasible to prepare elaborate mausoleums to enable the rich middle class to migrate safely into the next world. Finally it became technically feasible to prepare all of humanity for entering into the afterlife. This occurred at year zero. The concept of a cosmic intellectual integrity governing all Universe that is utterly concerned only with all humans which cosmic integrity, if properly worshipped and served, could arrange for the happy afterlife of every devout believer inspired inception of a plurality of new people's religions and two millennia of church, cathedral, temple and mosque building. In addition to getting all "worthy" people into the next world, ever-multiplying technical know-how made it successively feasible to take care of the present life, first of kings (divine right of kings), then nobles (magna carta), then of the well-to-do middle class (Victorian period) and in the twentieth century for all humanity. This eliminated the necessity for two worlds—one universe now embraced all.

STONE 18

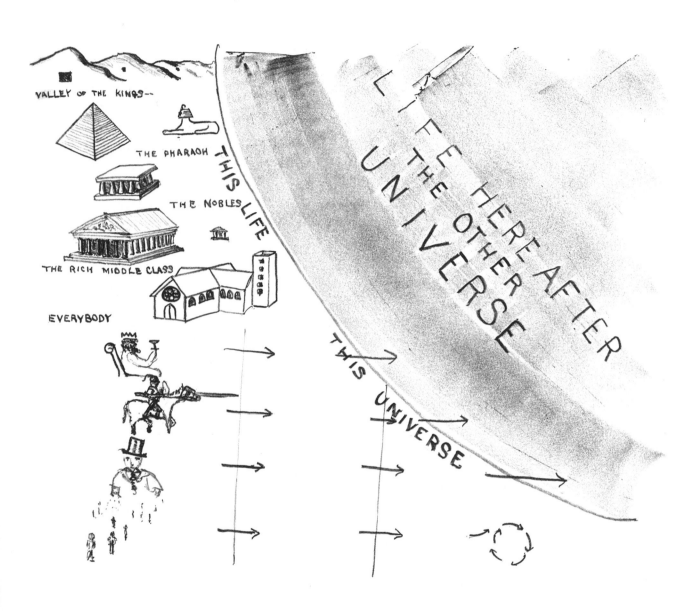

VALLEY OF THE KINGS--

THE PHARAOH

THE NOBLES LIFE

THIS LIFE

THE RICH MIDDLE CLASS

EVERYBODY

THIS UNIVERSE

LIFE HEREAFTER THE OTHER UNIVERSE

There arose a philosophic necessity to evolve a common people's God who could and would welcome everybody into the afterlife. About 600 years prior to this, Buddha, an Indochina prince, renounced his royal claim on the throne and promulgated the concept of a cosmic intellectual integrity governing all Universe that is utterly concerned only with all humans, which cosmic integrity, if properly worshipped and served, could arrange for the happy after-life of every devout believer. Employing the generally developed stone temple-building capability and thereby the feasibility of physically gratifying the common peoples' superstitious yearning for access to the sublime vs. hellish afterlife by production of temples and a priest-hood that would directly address the needs and problems of all "good" people, the east-west trading masters proceeded to import into Asia Minor the by-then-well-developed, pro-plebeian, concerned philosophy of 600 years earlier, naturally born Buddha but under new names and clothed in a variety of new and unique legends adjusted to the difference in everyday experiences of Occidental vs. Oriental people, of which Orientals the Occidental people had no knowledge whatsoever, it being of vast advantage to the east-west trade masters that neither the west nor the east people should have any knowledge of how they might obtain anything they needed except through the traders' monopoly.

Following the Egyptian and Babylonian priests' invention of the beginnings of humanity in the Garden of Eden and its coincidence with the dawning awareness of a potential afterlife for all those who disciplined themselves to live a God-fearing and worshipping life, various codes of conduct were religiously evolved in many areas of the Near East throughout the whole millennium, during which it was becoming progressively evident and popularly thinkable that not only was it feasible to provide means for getting the great ruler—as in the first dynasties of Egypt—into the next world and later also the nobles—as in the second set of dynasties of Egypt—and even later of getting in all the rich middle class—as in the late Greek and early Roman era—but the time had now come when it was feasible for all humanity to qualify for entry into the eternal happiness of the afterlife. In the Egyptian, east-west-water-route-mastering world we have Moses (illegitimate son of a princess, ergo, like Buddha of royal stock) found floating in a basket in the bullrush swamp. Moses matures, counsels, and leads the common people, in contradistinction to the middle class or the nobles or the pharaoh, who would resent and resist sharing their exclusive afterlife prerogatives with the common people. Moses leads them out of their enslavement by the rich power structure of trade route 10 into a new promised land, that of trade route 9.

Under the dawning awareness of the feasibility of accommodating all humanity's entrance into the next world, many scriptures were progressively written which adopted the composite history-won wisdom, philosophy, and experience of the East into Western comprehendibility and identified that philosophy and divine disclosure exclusively with a special living individual, a prophet, a savior, speaking with the authority of God as a native son of the Western World's lands and peoples. Though Buddha, Christ, and Mohammed are each scriptured as being one unique, living individual, it is probable that each constituted an idealized composite individual, possessed of and professing the comprehensive quintessence of then evolving philosophy, cosmology, and mysticism. It is probable that there were many like-minded and identically committed humans, each one of whom might have been the central figure upon which the "official" character of their prophets was built.

After the legend of Moses the lawgiver a consortium consisting of the two Samarkand trade routes masters conglomerating with the Crete-Egypt-Red-Sea water route "world" trade masters, operating under the code name "the three wise men of the east," hopeful of gaining the largest popular market control in Asia Minor, invented an even more uniquely born prophet bespeaking a Westernized adaptation of the Buddhist concepts whose miraculous birth by a virgin in Bethlehem close by Jerusalem, and whose sojourn in the wilderness, preaching, being betrayed and crucified, whose martyrdom, resurrection from the dead, and ascent into Heaven (from just outside Jerusalem) did indeed capture public acceptance far beyond the hope of its conceivers and powerfully enough eventually to command the dating of all world affairs from the new Western prophet's theoretical birthdate.

Five hundred years later, shaken by the success of the three wise men's syndicate, operating trade route 7 from China via the Indian Ocean, Persian Gulf, Baghdad, Euphrates and caravan, their southernmost, routes-5-and-6-primarily-horse-mounted-overland competitors through the Khyber Pass and Kashmir, invented their prophet, who was much more like Buddha, was more realistically born in Mecca of mortal parents, was a wealthy but wise merchant who in his maturity went into the wilderness and evolved approximately the same Orient-evolved, comprehensively integrated all-history philosophy, and though making his birthplace, Mecca, the capital of his religious followers, did himself go to Jerusalem, where he competed in the ascent-into-Heaven event.

Thus did the successive northerly vs. southerly trade route masters alter history to suit their purposes. Thus for instance was the Roman Emperor Constantine puppeted into shifting Empire headquarters to the command city of the Bosphorus to re-establish the northernmost overland east-west trade route and to service the new greater European trade market reached by the Aegean, Adriatic, and Mediterranean waters by the (Pho)necian-(Ve)netian merchant ships. Thus one trade route mastery yielded to another as accomplished by the omni-ingenuity of the competitive route masters. The "Holy Grail" drive of the "Crusaders" was undertaken by the water traders hopeful of wresting from the horse-mounted Moslem-Saracens the control of both the Mesopotamian and Suez access to the Red Sea and Persian Gulf and therewith to the Arabian and Indian ocean trade routes.

Suddenly all ten of these Near East-transiting, overland or overseas, Orient-to-Europe trade routes were altogether eclipsed when Henry the Navigator of Portugal inaugurated sailing all the way from Europe to the Orient via the North and South Atlantic, around Africa to India and China. Thereafter a succession of European world-ocean masteries occurred which culminated in the East India Company's "British-Empire"-puppeted supremacy over all the world's oceanic trade routes. This oceanic mastery suddenly terminated in World War II, when the line-of-supply control shifted into the air, and is now shifting again into the airless ocean of outer nothingness, intervening relativity's cosmic events.

TRICAP 19

Goldy now elucidates some post-Eden history for the bears. Mycenae was able to control the floatable line of supply to besiege the static walls of Troy. Homer's epic probably represents the first introduction to public knowledge of the changeover in the grand strategy of the world's power structure from supreme dependence on the power of the almost invincibly massive high walls of the great city-states to supreme dependence on the naval architects' engineeringly superior control of the lines of supply by deep sea vessels—the waters covering three quarters of planet earth reached all the river mouths of all continents and islands, outperforming the separate land-terminalled overland routes. For long the local, fertile lands commanding, city-states masters had starved the famished outsiders to death. Now the more-with-lessing Mycenean sea masters starved the Trojan city-state insiders because the Trojans were the progeny of the overland horsemen, the Mycenean sailormen produced the famous Trojan Horse within which symbol of seeming acknowledgement of Trojan superiority they hid some fighting men while deceptively withdrawing their maritime fleet.

Goldy and the bears soliloquize on the fact that this 2000 B.C. historically lethal moment of conversion of supremacy from absolute dominance by massiveness to a doing-more-with-less mastery marked the beginning of a four-millennia development that would culminate at the end of the twentieth century A.D. in doing so much with so little as finally to be able to support all humans at an economically sustainable higher standard of living than any have ever experienced, thus to eliminate altogether the fundamental scarcity syndrome and all lethal interstruggling of humanity, allowing humanity to become preoccupied with greater problems of Universe, with which ultimately to cope, humans had been given their minds.

STONE 19

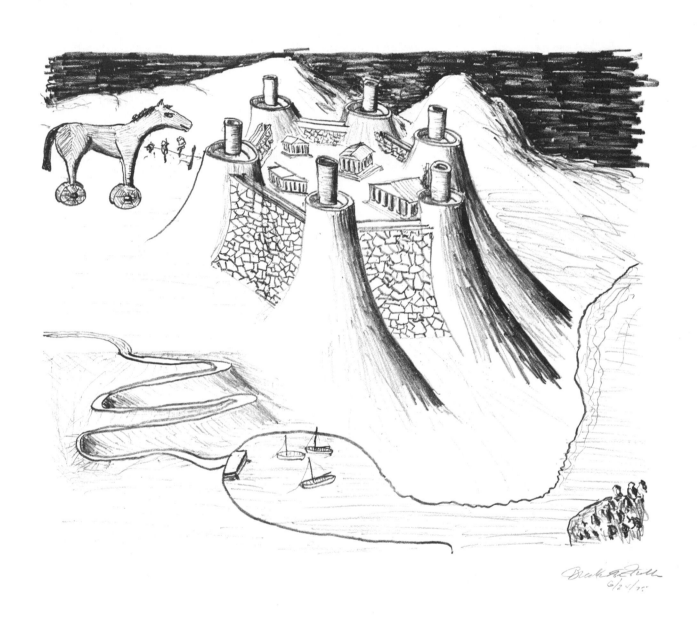

Goldy now elucidates some other post-Eden history for the bears. She notes that allied with ancient Crete and its sea power, Mycenae was a very successful city-state, so successful as to have developed the additional capability of building ships and going to sea. Its peoples were able to control the floatable line of supply to besiege the static walls of Troy. While much of the history of Greece and the Greek islands is symptomatic, Homer's epic probably represents the first introduction to public knowledge of the changeover in the grand strategy of the world's power structure from supreme dependence on the power of the almost invincibly massive high walls of the great city-states to supreme dependence on the engineeringly superior control of the lines of supply at sea.

The higher and bigger the walls, the more secure had the city-states' human insiders felt themselves to be. Economic mastery of the world affairs by the mobile, more-with-lessing, comparatively frail wooden ships of the sea gradually overwhelmed the local land monarchs' massively inert static-states' security. For long the local, fertile-lands-commanding, city-state masters had starved the famished outsiders to death. Now the sea masters starved the city-state insiders to death.

Goldy and the bears soliloquize on the fact that this 2000 B.C. historically lethal moment of conversion of supremacy from absolute dominance by massiveness to a doing more with less mastery marked the beginning of a four-millennia development that would culminate at the end of the twentieth century A.D. in doing so much with so little as finally to be able to support all humans at an economically sustainable higher standard of living than any have ever experienced, thus to eliminate altogether the fundamental scarcity syndrome and all lethal interstruggling of humanity; allowing humanity to become preoccupied with greater problems of Universe, with which ultimately to cope, humans had been given their minds.

After the fall of Troy the most astute Orient overland survivors of the great land barons who had originally masterminded the evolution of the city-state, finding themselves physically overwhelmed by the fleets and the armed sailors' control of the line of supply, evolved a new counterstrategy for much more subtly besting the sea-power people. They realized that (1) the

114

ships had to be built and repaired on the land and (2) that the cargoes had to be loaded and unloaded on the land, preferably at the land barons' vanquished city ports. So a coterie of the smartest of the old city-state "brains" finessed the military debacle by inventing the concept of finance and tempting the sea-power people to borrow on their "credit" to build new and larger ships as well as to "finance" the "purchasing" power of merchandise on their voyages, all accomplished through "credit" advanced to the sailormen by the old city-staters' "wealthy," who organized a showy bluff of secretly possessing vast resources of materials and labor which they had opportunistically finagled from others through intrigue, alluring promises, coercions, and conspiracies, and their invention of a new wealth of metallic coinage consisting of thick bronze bracelets in the general shape of a joined-together pair of curved bull horns, the common symbol of the Minoan Cretans, Vikings, and Phoenicians, to be used as trading monies in lieu of the former cattle carried in their ships of trade. This converted the concept of wealth from true life-support-producing substance to abstract symbols betokening the awesome power of the monarchs, whose sculpted portraits appeared on the coins which succeeded the bronze bull-horn bracelets. They also changed the written language of trade, which theretofore had been dominated by the Oriental ideographs and picture writing in general, which had pictured whole concepts. For this they substituted the phonetic, or sound-symbol writing, which events coincide with the Tower of Babel and the loss of general human communication based on universally identical visual experiences. Thus began a game of poker in which for almost 4,000 years the finance masters held and dealt their mystique cards and avoided having to show their own hands, which indeed became rich in time as they introduced ever-lower-intrinsic-value paper money and time-lag accounting at ever-higher interest rates and ever-more-intricate discounting and rediscounting at ever-higher frequency of "turnover," which with the nineteenth-century advent of the telegraph, world-around cables, and eventually wireless made possible their twenty-four-hour use of both depositors' and "in-transit" monies in world-around financial markets.

Thereafter the financially powerful leaders evolved a comprehensive scheme of specialized education that would keep all individuals of society "minding only their own business," while the masters and their financiers minded everybody's business. The more complex human affairs became, the more "turnover" and brokerage fees accrued. Thus the master strategists came to finance a divide-and-conquer educational system through which the power-wielding masters instruct their scientists and others on how to become highly paid, faithful, specialized, and unquestioning servants. The scientists are told to confine their concerns within the internal affairs of their expensive laboratories—there to lay the "eggs," the disposition of which must be left unquestioningly to the wisdom of their patron masters, whose superior wisdom was, and as yet is, assumed to be manifest and inherent in the hard fact of the masters' ultimately weapons-backed, no-intrinsic-value-paper accounted, superior eco-political power.

In view of all the foregoing Goldy and the bears agree that the Austronesian water people constitute the prime ongoing organism of human evolution designed and conditioned by multimillion years of experience to withstand the mania of rationalized selfishness and eventually capable through ever-more-with-less artifacts of rendering altogether obsolete opportunistic myopia in general. The water people cannot pretend to themselves, as do the businessmen, that a rectangle is an inherently stable structure, that the wind, sun, or any other operating facilities of Universe belong to anyone, or that there exists seemingly forever a lethal inadequacy of human life support purportedly inherent in the metabolics of planet earth's biospheric system. This is a syndrome of money-makers, which with the comprehensive human mind's exclusively artifact produced more-with-lessing is, as we shall see, now becoming patently invalid. So clearly is it in evidence to the comprehensively informed that the now-known-to-be-recirculating metallic resources and daily cosmic energy income and the present level of technological know-how of earthians are more than adequate by a factor of four to one for sustaining support of all humanity and all their foreseeable generations to come at a higher standard of living than any humans have thus far in history ever before experienced—and to do so within only one decade.

The fundamental planetary scarcity syndrome can now, in the last half of the twentieth century, be maintained only by the year-after-year-continuing, incredible waste of the 200 billion dollars a year spent by the world's leading powers on armament and ammunition, spying and counterspying, contrived rioting, psycho-guerilla warfaring, civilian bombings, narcotics pushing on one another, assassinations, murder, wrecking homes and devastating the countrysides of unfortunate people and countries chosen by the "socialists" and "capitalists" for further conduct of their continuous exploratory warfaring by arming, training, and financing their respective puppet "enemies," thus avoiding direct confrontation of one another by the principal ideological adversaries, which engagement could not be terminated by negotiation. Two hundred billion dollars a year for the last quarter-century totals five trillion dollars which since World War II have been deliberately wasted by the world's power structures to fortify their respective political stances "taken" in relation to the fallacious sociopolitical assumption of fundamental life-support inadequacy, in respect to which each ideology says, "You may not like my system, but it is the fairest and most logical way of coping with lethally inadequate life support."

We have politics and war only because of the "lethal scarcity" syndrome. Politics, war, weaponry, and deceit become obsolete with the world's discovery that through intellect's exponentially multiplying know-how and the latter's again exponentially multiplying more-with-less production and service-capabilities, including continual recirculation of the physical materials, there is now indeed an abundant capability to support and to accommodate all humanity if it stops wasting its resources for military purposes and for exclusively one-sided monetary and political profits.

As long as humanity has been convinced of the existence on our planet of an unalterable, lethal human-life-support inadequacy, just so long is selfishness to be rationalized as being not only "realistic" but essential in securing the vital needs of those dependent upon the family "bread-winner" or "bean guardian." Those who eschew selfishness and commit themselves to the golden rule are considered to be either ignorant or foolish.

Since, however, it is now looming into ever more widely held knowledge that there is and can continue to be ample life support for all, both today and tomorrow, for the first time in three million years of known human presence on this planet, selfishness can no longer be rationalized as inherently valid.

This is one of the most dramatic changes in all history. It is thus seen that the realism of the water people and their cosmically cultivated wisdom may again integrate synergetically to lead into noncompetitive, cosmically designed functioning of humanity as instrument-informed and exclusively mind-determined local Universe problem solvers; with limited but progressively enlightening access to the cosmic laws and design concepts that guarantee the integrity of eternally regenerative Universe.

Goldy and the bears note that since the fall of ancient Troy and establishment of supremacy of "the lines of supply," except for the subtle intrusion of the "business" man's complex credit and finance accounting system, there has been no fundamental change in the grand economic strategy of the power structure governing world affairs throughout the intervening 5,000 years. Whoever has controlled the line of supply has dominated. But the controlling of the line of supply has come to include the air fleets and the rocketry-delivered intercontinental atomic bombs, extraterrestrial space platforms, and super-sensing-spy satellites, all omni-electromagnetically guided with pinpoint accuracy by the instruments of a now ninety-nine percent invisible reality.

The scientific discovery or technical invention of ways of "doing more with less" constitutes the most highly "classified" of secret information of the most powerfully armed political states. Which side is going to demonstrate the most capability in doing more-with-the-same or more-with-less is the surprise factor that will "tip the scales" one way or the other as the war is joined and each side seems to match exactly the other's numbers and tons of ships, guns, and personnel at all strategic points. Because all the governments hold all such information secret, society fails to realize that there is a swiftly accelerating accomplishment of the more-with-lessing.

Swiftly recapitulating the epochal change in human affairs, Goldy repeats that hidden from society by the "top-secret" classification of both the super military giants of our planet, all inadvertently their power struggle has introduced so many ways of doing so much more with so much less investment of pounds of material, ergs of energy, and seconds of time per each task accomplished while ever increasing the range, power, and incisiveness of the performance that it is now technically and economically demonstratable that both the comprehensive physical and metaphysical know-how resources of the world are abundantly adequate to support all of humanity at a higher standard of living than any humans have ever known and to do so by 1985, provided those world resources are employed with the same new design ingenuity as that going into the conceptioning, development, and production of the top-cover warplanes of 1976 as compared with the technical complexity and production efficiency that went into producing the swords, saddles, harness, and uniforms of 1905's horse cavalry, which seventy years ago had the same world-around supreme cover function in land warfaring as have aircraft today.

The "business" man's business and its invention of abstract banking credit, finance, interest, deposits, coinage, economics, foreign exchange rates, balance of trade, insurance, bookkeeping, and above all uncontrolled "pricing" obviously prosper most when "goods" are scarcest. Scarcities are most certain of occurring when governments spend the most on armament production, which production tends to render scarce all peaceful life-support items and services. It becomes obvious why no book on economics ever mentions "doing more with less." "More with lessing" is thought to be by many paramount to giving more and better goods and services for ever lower prices, whereas money-making business is enchanted only with giving subtly ever less for ever higher prices. It is obvious why the stock market prices climb whenever the prospects loom for more war preparation or for relaxation of any restraints upon selfish exploitation of the many for the greater advantaging of the few.

Throughout all the three and one-half million years during which humans now are known to have been aboard planet earth, none knew that humanity had an option of total economic successes. Therefore, the selfish viewpoint has always been rationalizably justified. As yet known only to less than one percent of world people, humanity nonetheless has now come into a new relationship with Universe—a relationship wherein the cause of the struggle to survive economically has been approximately dispensed with.

TRICAP 20

Goldy says that with the first coinages of humanity now being brought out from Mediterranean ocean bottoms, one of the most frequent is that of the Phoenician sailor's symbol—the double-headed, two-way-facing Janus whose overall contour is that of the Cretan king's symbol, the vertical-axis hexagon. Dry-land anthropologists and archaeologists have misinterpreted the Janus symbol as meaning only that the sailor was a notorious liar, professing to be going one way but actually going the other. To the maritime archaeologists and anthropologists the Janus symbol clearly reveals that the sailors knew that they could face in any direction and, traveling constantly in that great-circle direction, come back to where they started because the earth is a sphere. The sailor's symbol was the six-triangle hexagon, for only triangles are structurally stable. With their keeled, triangularly trussed framing and triangularly rigged ships, navigators have encircled the spherical earth for aeons. Land people have been historically local and ignorantly subservient to the earth's sphericity, commencing their wall buildings with stone, the land-holding and -guarding people build compressively, squarely, redundantly and heavily, commencing their shipbuilding with wood, water people build tensively, curvilinearly, triangularly, and with utmost efficiency of realized function per each ounce of weight, minute of time, and erg of energy designedly invested in their "environment controlling" vessels. They must do ever more with ever less in order to float controllably in any manner of storms while doing so much with so relatively little.

STONE 20

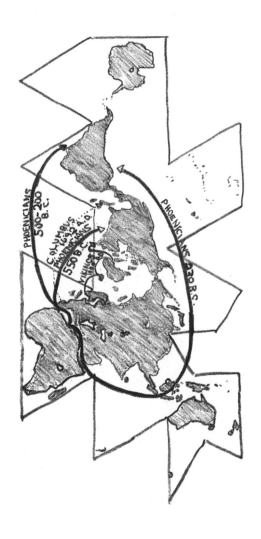

121

When the majority of humans have learned that this is so, evolution will allow earthians to become preoccupied with Universe in an entirely new way—the way of the child. Quoting Goldy's friend Christopher Morley's 1922 poem:

> The poetry, innate, untold,
> of being only four years old.
>
> Still young enough to be a part
> of nature's great impulsive heart,
> born comrade of bird, beast and tree
> and unselfconscious as the bee—
>
> and yet with lovely reason skilled
> each day new paradise to build,
> elate explorer of each sense,
> without dismay, without pretense!
>
> In your unstained, transparent eyes
> there is no conscience, no surprise:
> life's queer conundrums you accept,
> your strange divinity still kept.

Goldy also recalls that until the twentieth century reality was everything humans could touch smell, hear, and see. The twentieth century was opened with discovery of the electron, radio, and electromagnetics in general. Now 99.9 percent of the ranges of reality within which humanity operates informally and incisively are nondirectly apprehendable by the human senses. In any room anywhere around planet earth there are nonsensorially more than two million radio programs which can be tuned in upon and transformed into direct apprehending by human senses. Indoors or outdoors anywhere around earth, if you have the right radio set, you can tune in a program being broadcast around the earth from an orbiting satellite equipped with sensors that can report to you on a television screen where every live beef cattle on earth is located and how many there are of them. This is the new reality, whose total synergetic significance is as yet utterly uncomprehended by humanity. This new reality can only be coped with by the scientifically and technically trained brains and fearless use of the latter by human minds.

Implicit in its exponential rate of information growth by inclusion and refinement is the inference that evolution is about to render all humanity both economically successful and omni-intercooperative as people forget yesterday's struggle and yield to the fascination of the new functioning in Universe which humans were deliberately designed to perform with competence.

"Certain it is," says Goldy, "that entirely unforeseen by any, the same factors of evolution that during only the first three quarters of the twentieth century have transformed humanity from an omni-isolated to an omni-integrated planetary relationship and from a condition of 99 percent poverty and destitution to a condition in which more than 52 percent of all world's peoples are enjoying a standard of living far superior to that of any monarch of all history up to the opening of the twentieth century, while concurrently doubling their life span, will go on to produce progressive advancement of human life support and "expectancy" at the rate already established, which clearly promises total physical success for all humanity before the close of the twentieth century. This unheralded event has been utterly transcendental to any of humanity's political or economic planning. Within only one century humanity will have been transformed from a condition of local, ignorant self-survival preoccupation to an awareness of the omni-interrelated and omni-interdependent ecology not only of planet earth but of omni-regenerative universe itself."

TRICAP 21

Goldy and the bears agree that the Austronesian water people constitute the prime ongoing organism of human evolution designed and conditioned by multimillion years of experience to withstand the mania of rationalized selfishness and eventually capable through ever-more-with-ever-less artifacts of rendering altogether obsolete opportunistic myopia in general. The water people cannot pretend to themselves, as do the businessmen, that a rectangle is an inherently stable structure, that the wind, sun, or any other operating facilities of Universe belong to anyone, or that there exists a seemingly forever lethal inadequacy of human life support purportedly inherent in the metabolics of planet earth's biospheric system.

As long as humanity has been convinced of the existence on our planet of an unalterable, lethally human-life-support inadequacy, just so long is selfishness to be rationalized as being not only "realistic" but essential in securing the vital needs of those dependent upon the family "bread-winner" or "bean guardian," those who eschew selfishness and commit themselves to the golden rule are considered to be either ignorant or foolish. Since, however, it is now looming into ever more widely held knowledge that there is and can continue to be ample life support for all, both today and tomorrow, for the first time in three million years of known human presence on this planet, selfishness can no longer be rationalized as inherently valid. This is one of the most dramatic changes in all history.

STONE 21

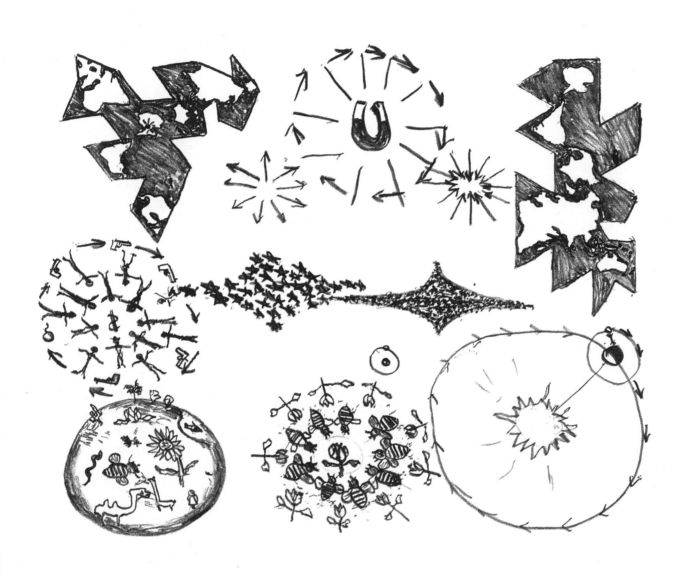

So Goldy draws a final scenario picture for the bears. It shows them how cosmic evolution gradually steers humans on earth into discovery, subsequent realistic heeding, and finally into deliberate local employment of the precessional governance not only of terrestrial affairs, but also of the omni-micro- and omni-macro-precessional behaviors of the billions of galaxies themselves.

Goldy's picture shows the bears how the cosmic ecology requirements are being met on our earth as demonstrated by the honey bee's chromosomally programmed 180-degree entrance into the flowers, while inadvertently (precessionally) bumbling at ninety degrees with its fuzzy tail to cross-pollinize the terrestrial vegetation. Goldy also draws a picture of all the honey-money-bee-people buzz-bumbling for honey profits in weaponry businesses which inadvertently (precessionally) cross-pollinize development of the ever-more-with-less accomplishments, the again inadvertent "fall-outs" which ultimately produce a high standard of living for all earthians—not with high standards of living as a prime objective, but only in order to utterly subordinate any further deferment of adoption of completely feasible metabolic operation efficiency. This subordination brings into full consideration and sustained realization the prime functioning of human minds as local Universe problem solvers operating in consonance with the integrity of omni-regenerative, never unitarily conceptual, ever synergetically intriguing and refreshing Scenario Universe.

Big Bear soliloquizes, "Goldy—all that you have been thinking with us thoroughly summarizes the main historical threads and trendings of the latest cosmic attempts to establish one of our myriad of already successfully operative, mind-conducted, information-gathering, and local-Universe problem-solving stations, this one within the solar system. Gestation of such a planting and its evolutionary cultivation requires multimillions of years and employment of the full gamut of generalized principles.

"When Universe has important complex functions to be made locally operative, and the complexity of their realization permits a high possibility of malfunctioning through local self-monitoring, then Universe makes more starts than the mathematically indicated number of probable failures for the degree of complex evolution involved. From our sky advantage we have witnessed a number of multimillion-year attempts to establish the planet earth mind station. Every time it nears successful realization, the residual ignorance-sustained fear factor, plus the momentum of once necessary but no longer required selfishness prolongs successful emergence from the historical wombs of permitted ignorance within which humanity had been metabolically gestated by a sufficient abundance of life-support phenomena to permit all the only-by-trial-and-error-gainable discoveries of the cosmic principles, and thereby discovery of the significance of human mind, and thereby discovery of the human function in Universe to be realized only by emergence from the motherwomb to function on its own metaphysical integrity. "It is at this critical moment in the previous cosmic obstetrics that both fear and selfishness have pushed the omni-holocaust buttons, whose devastating transformations have required vast ages within which to re-organize and re-establish conditions under which new plantings and evolutionary cultivation may again be undertaken.

"But," says Big Bear, "Goldy, you have so ably comprehended and elucidated both the requirements and the options available for this solution that humans have now what appears to your celestial friends to be the thus-far-best chance of realizing their potentials."

To this Goldy thoughtfully responds, "If the grown-ups remain sufficiently preoccupied with their obsolete games of money and politics, the youth of humanity, disenchanted with the futility of selfishness, will quietly cooperate to control earthian affairs. The sensitivity of youth, its spontaneous truthfulness, its compassion, and above all its love-inspired drive to understand the great mysteries of human presence in Universe, will lead humanity to successful realization of its designed function in Universe. I am confident that you, my magnificent constellar friends, will witness a successful birth."

Goldy throws kisses to each of the bears, and all three bears respond to Goldy with a celestial "standing ovation" lasting for hours—an incredible brilliance of the Milky Way arching the sky from east to west ever and anon, helter-skeltered with shooting stars, with the whole northern sky surrounding the Three Bears pulsatingly radialled with the multicolored lights of an aurora borealis—all the while accompanied by a John Cage-inspiring symphonic masterpiece—the majestic silence of eternally regenerative cosmic integrity.

EPILEVER

WE ARE LOOKING THROUGH THE EYES
AND MIND OF A MAN
WHO HAS NEVER SEEN THE WORLD BEFORE
SEEING IT CONSTANTLY
SEEING IT COMPREHENSIVELY

BY CHALLENGING CONTINUALLY HOW HE KNOWS
WHAT HE KNOWS WE KNOW SO MUCH MORE

THE CLARITY OF IMAGES AND WORDS
SUGGESTS THAT THE BEGINNING OF WHAT BUCKY SEES
IS JUST BARELY VISIBLE
TO THE EXTENT OF THIS NEW INSIGHT
INTO HOW

OUR DREAMS NEED NOT BE THE EVIDENCE OF RESTLESS SLEEP
BUCKY'S QUEST IN WAKING HAS ENABLED US TO LIFT
OUR EYES AND FEEL IN MIND
THE WAVES OF POSSIBILITIES
THAT WITHOUT THIS NAVIGATOR
WOULD BREAK SILENTLY AT OUR PAST

TO READ THESE WORDS ON THE PAGE THE LINES ON THE PAPER
WHICH BUCKY HAS MAPPED SO DELICATELY
TAKES A PRESENCE
WHICH REACHES
FROM DEEP WITHIN THE PAPER AND INK AND PAGE
AND PROPELS THE SENSES AND THE IDEA

INTO THE MIND OF THE EYES
WITHOUT FALTERING   THIS COULD ONLY BE DONE
WHERE IT WAS DONE AT UNIVERSAL LIMITED ART EDITIONS
WITH TATYANA GROSMAN
WITH BILL GOLDSTON
WITH TONY TOWLE AND PAUL VIOLI
WITH JOHN LUND AND JUDA ROSENBERG,
JAMES V. SMITH, ANDREE JONES AND MIKI FUKUSHIMA

BUCKY WEAVES A STORY IN THE SKY
THROUGH THE STARS, IN THE OCEANS
ACROSS OUR KNOWLEDGE OF HISTORY
ABOUT OUR SENSE OF THE MEASURE OF EARTH
WITH THREADS WE NEVER
EVEN NOTICED
INTO A CLOTH WE CAN
USE IN ANY WHETHER

AS THE JOY OF ENERGY OF CHILDHOOD
HIS HANDS ON THE STONES
SIGNAL TO EACH OF US
TO DROP OUR IMAGINED BURDENS
AND DANCE

THROUGH THE LIFE AND MIND OF R. BUCKMINSTER FULLER HAS
JOURNEYED SOME OF THE MOST AMAZING ACTS OF UNDERSTANDING
WITNESSED HERE AS PRINTS NOT OF ROYALTY BUT THOSE WE ARE JUST
BEGINNING TO BE ABLE TO FOLLOW

EDWIN SCHLOSSBERG
1975